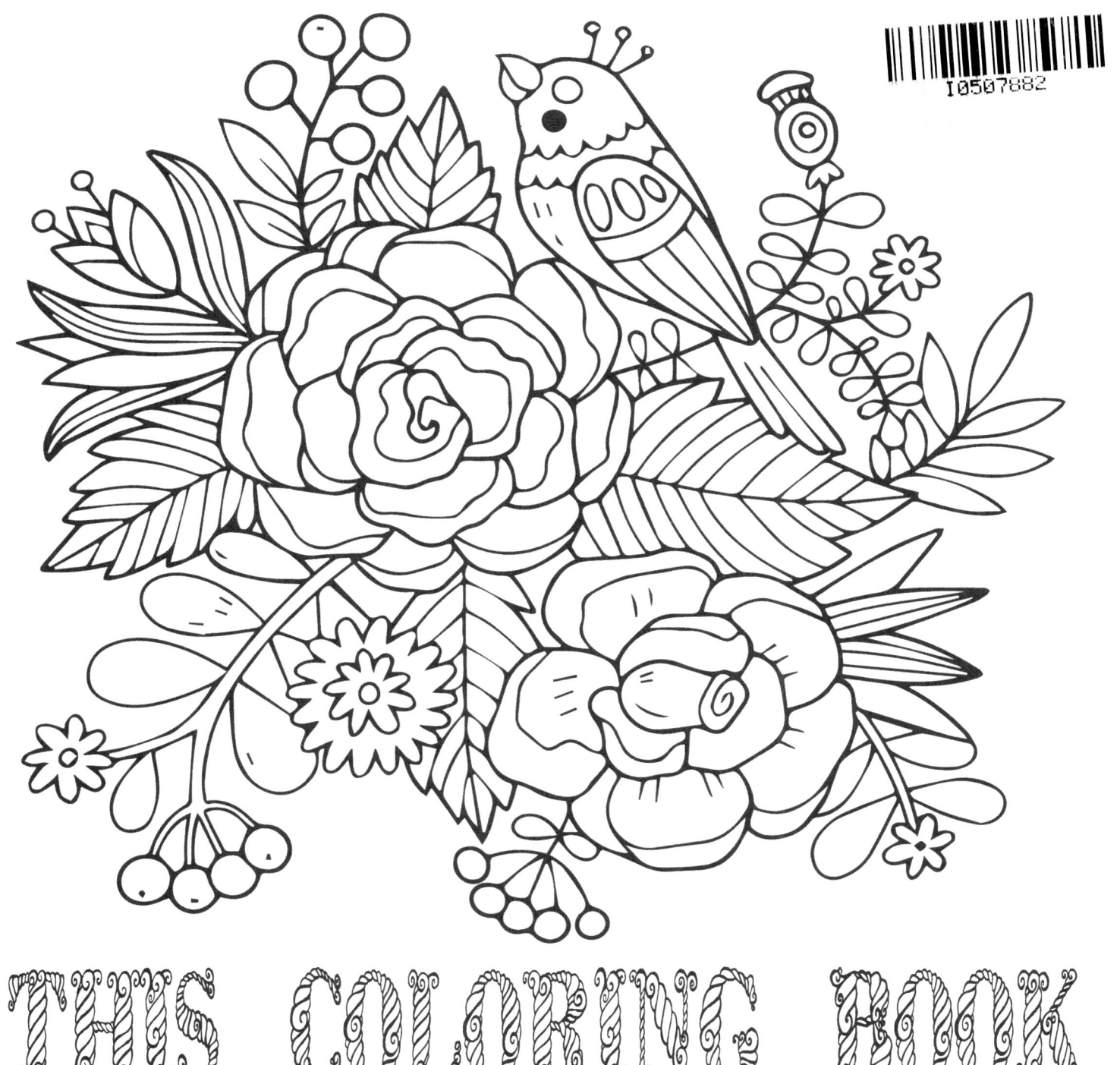

THIS COLORING BOOK BELONGS TO

THIS BOOK CONTAINS 34 SINGLE-SIDED MANDALAS COLORING PAGES FOR ADULTS. FRIENDLY FOR BEGINNERS AS THE PAGES WILL PROGRESS FROM EASY TO DIFFICULT LEVEL.

EVERY COLORING PAGE WILL PULL YOU INTO THE WORLD OF RELAXATION WHERE YOUR STRESS, PRESSURES, WORRIES, AND CONCERNS WILL BE FADING AWAY.

TEST YOUR ARTISTIC SKILLS AND LET YOUR CREATIVITY FLOWS.

This puzzles book created and copyright ©2020
By Grace Wright
All rights reserved

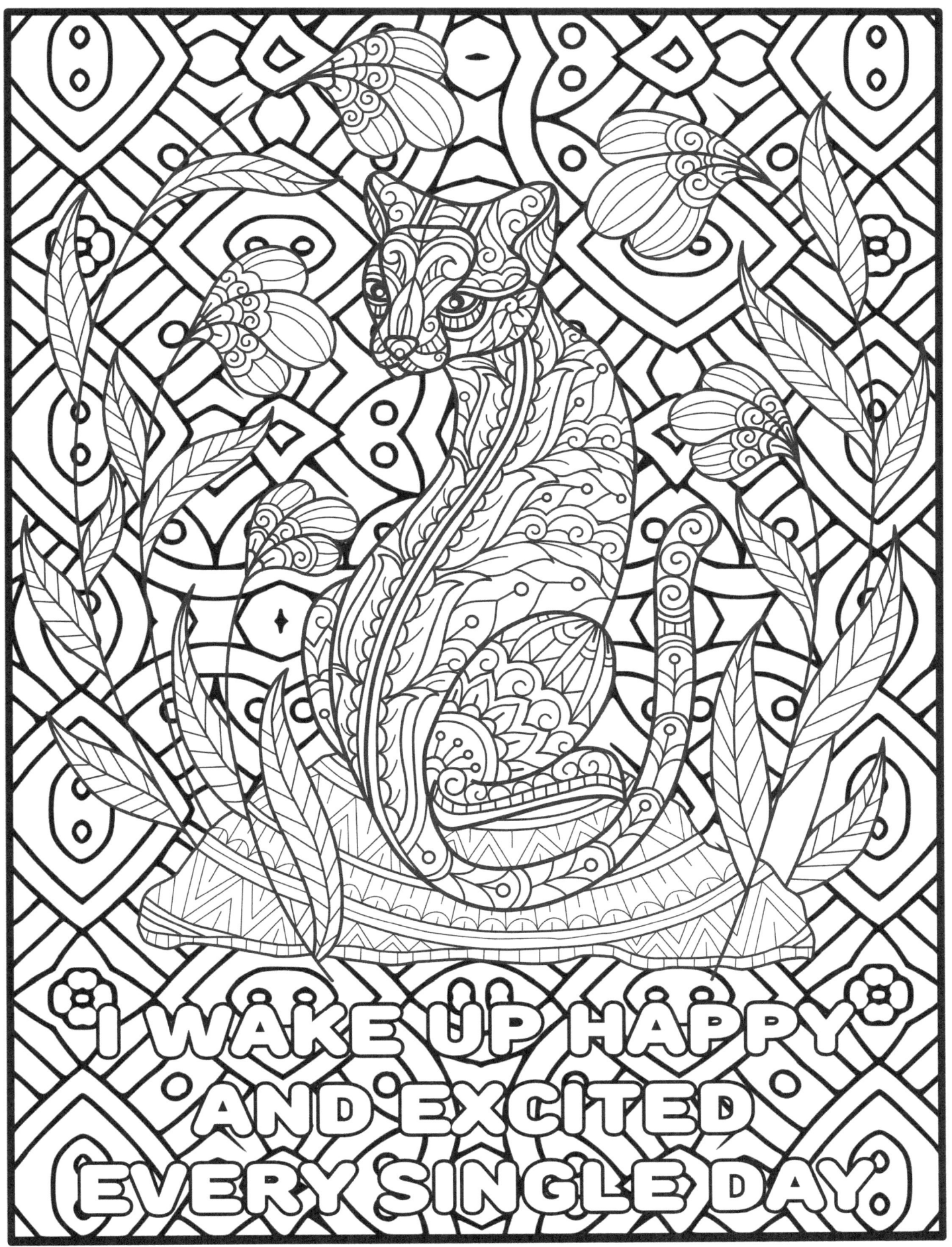

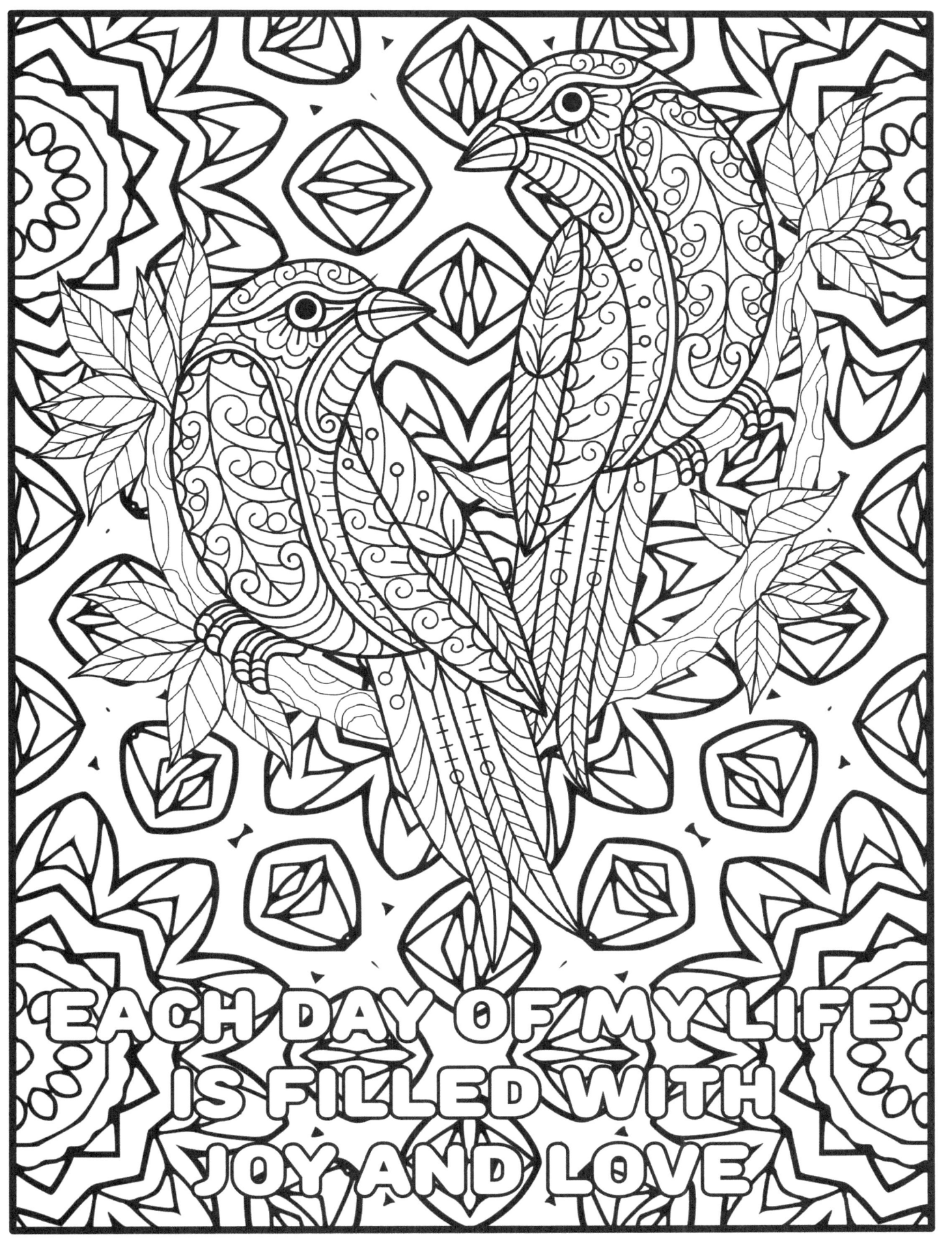

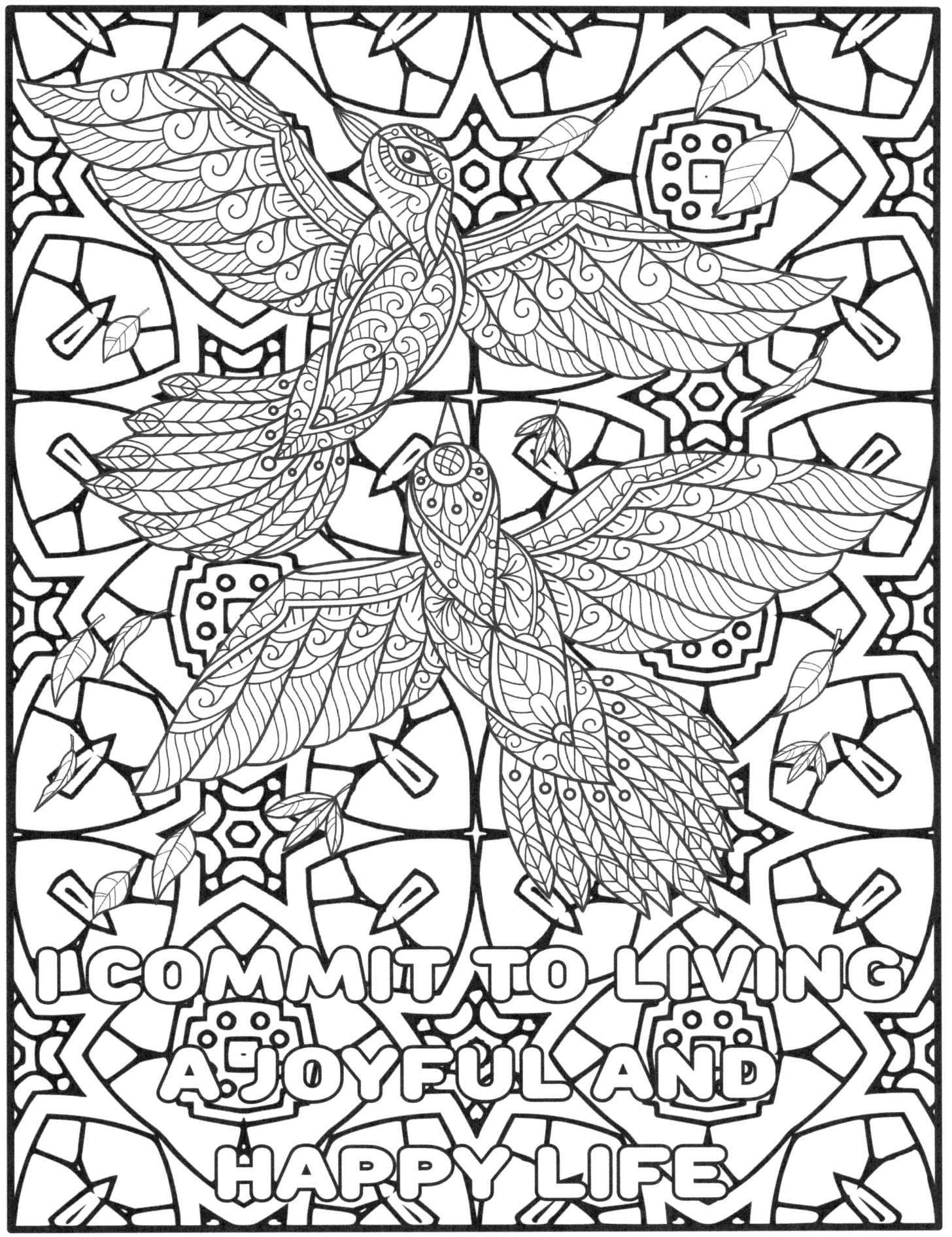

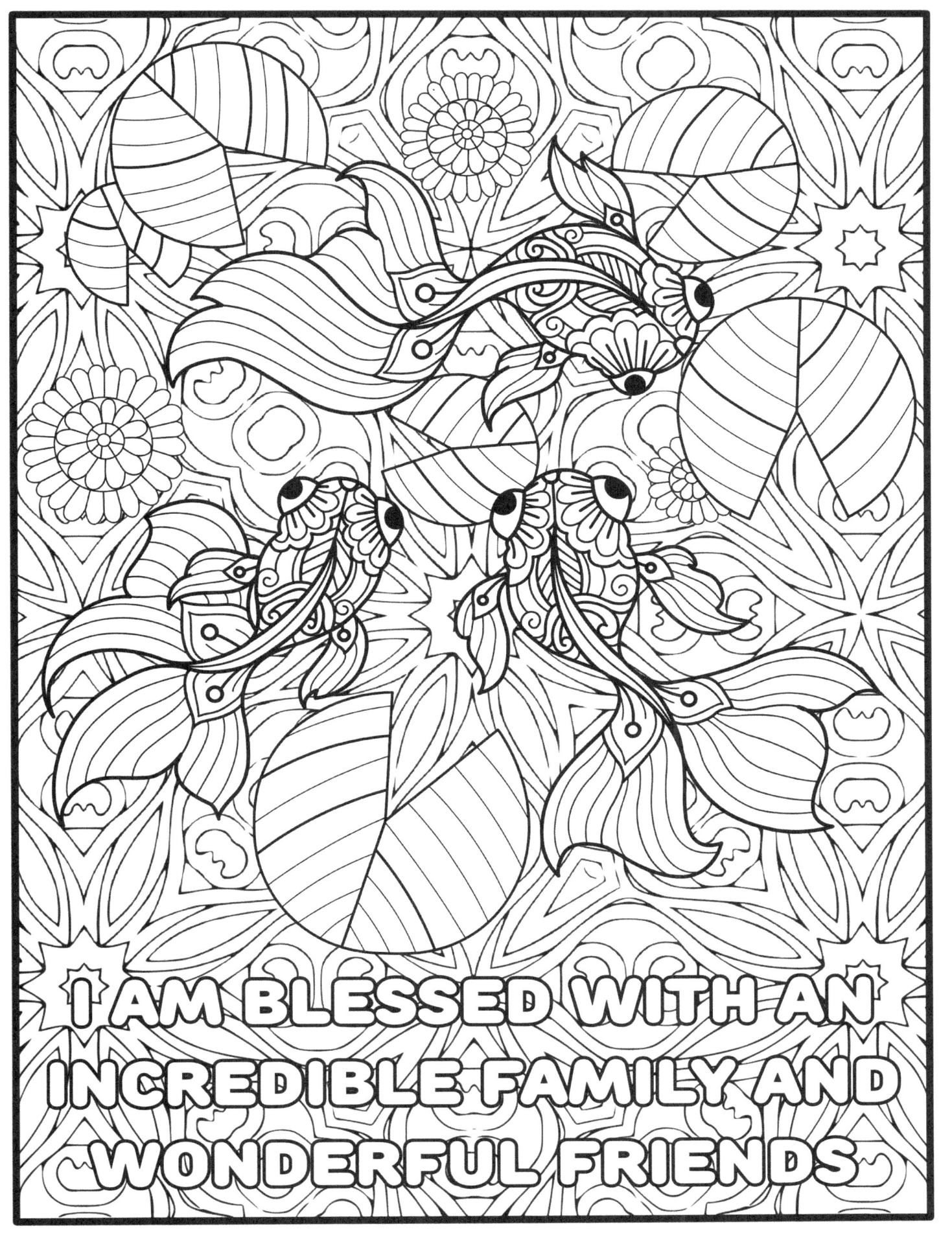

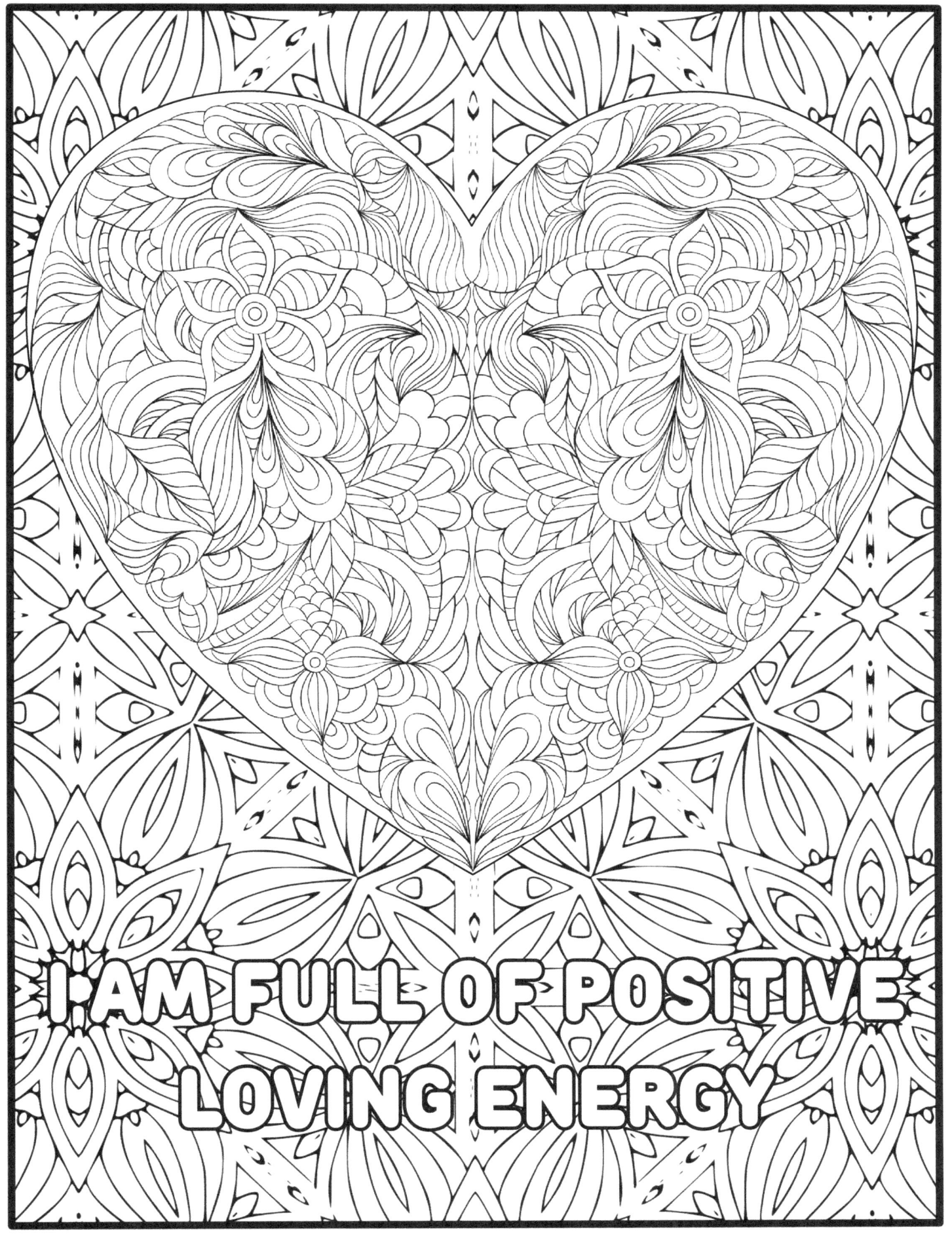

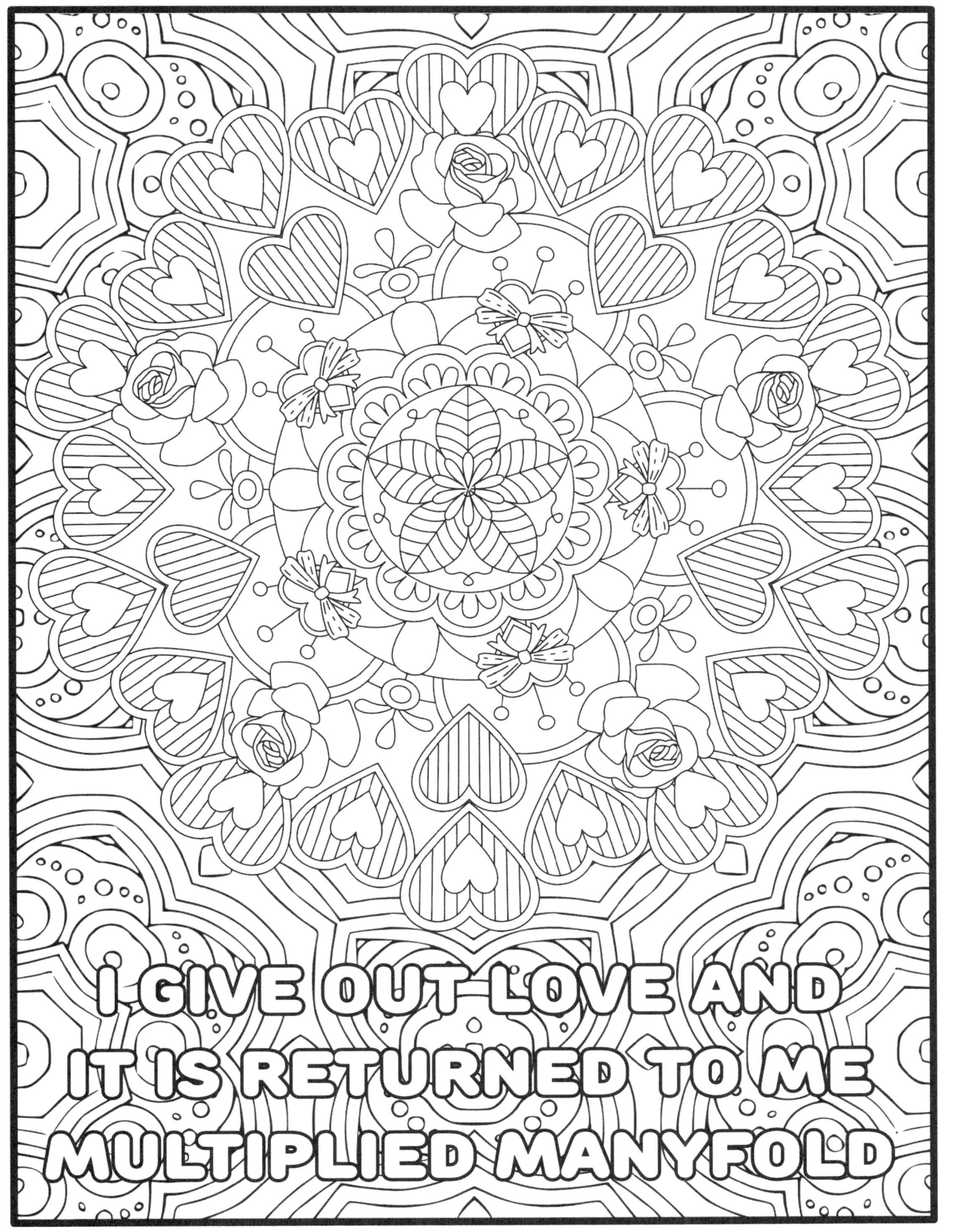

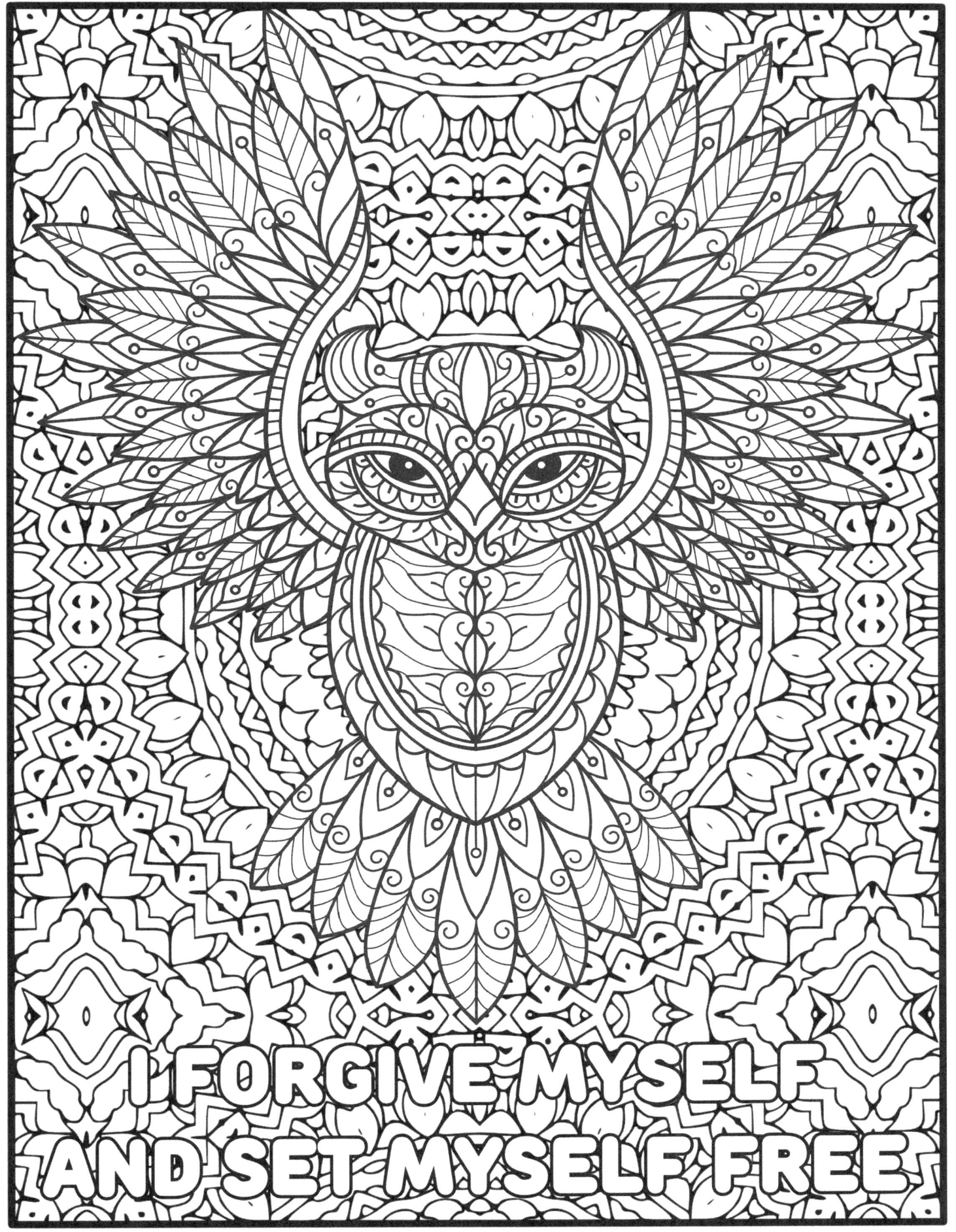

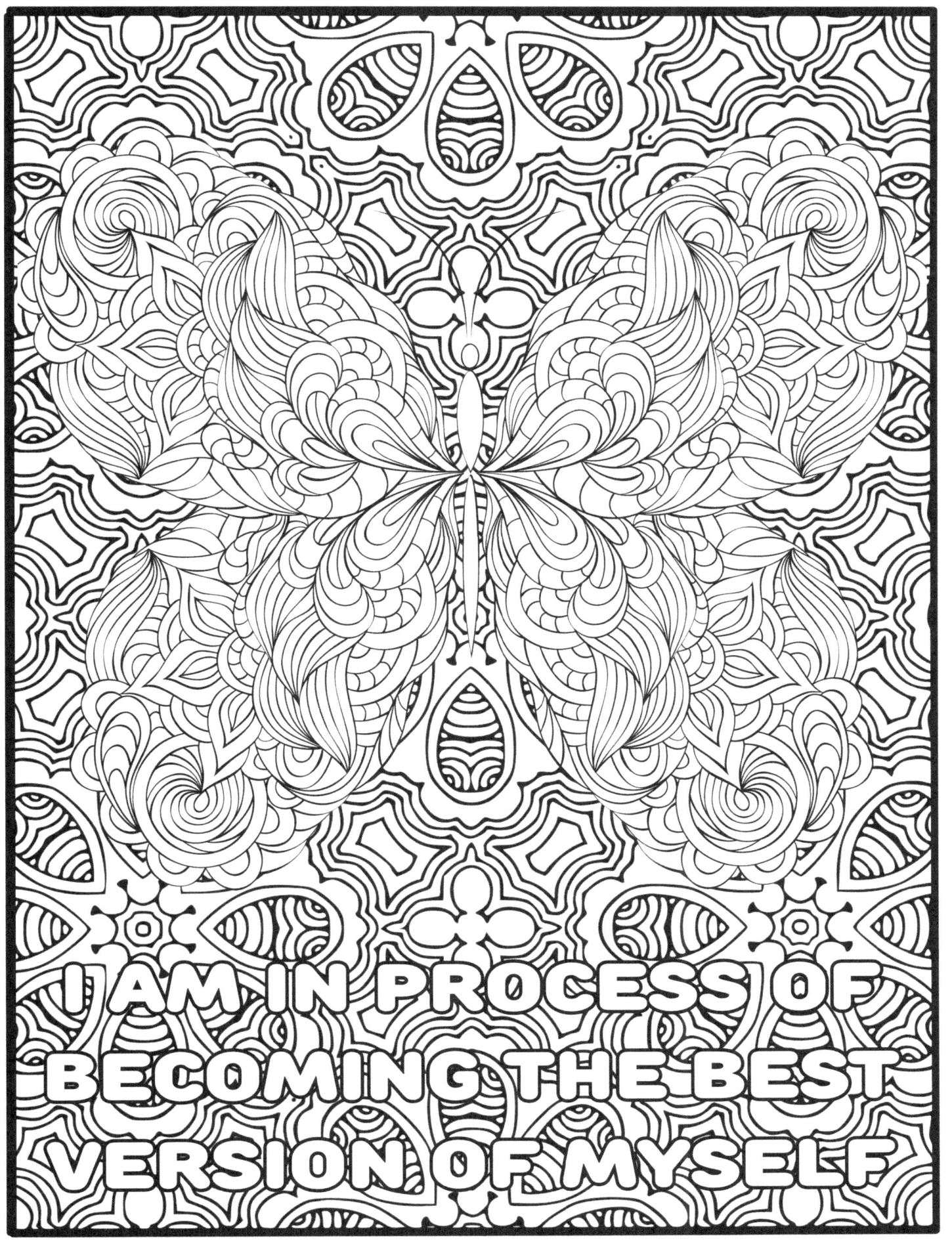

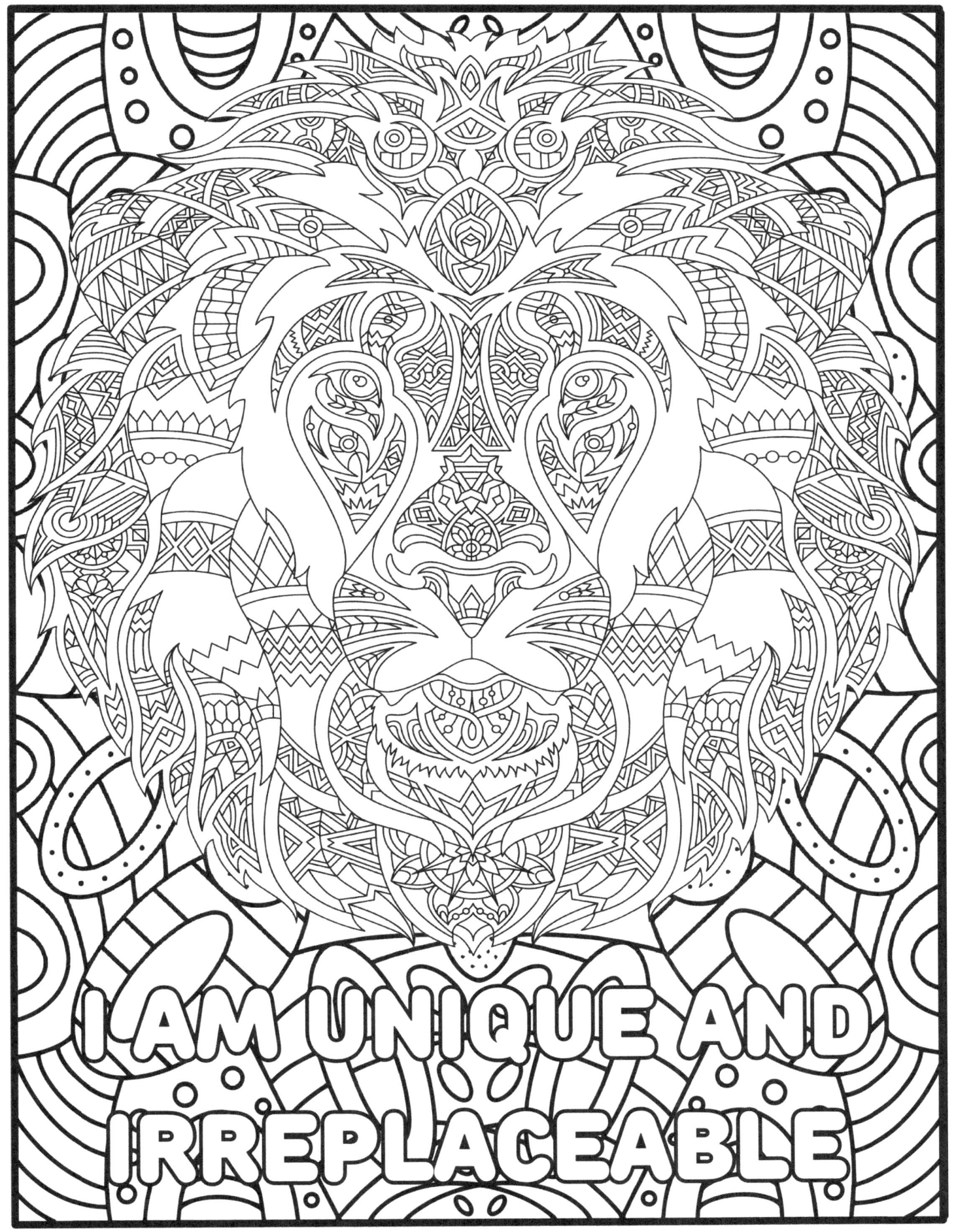

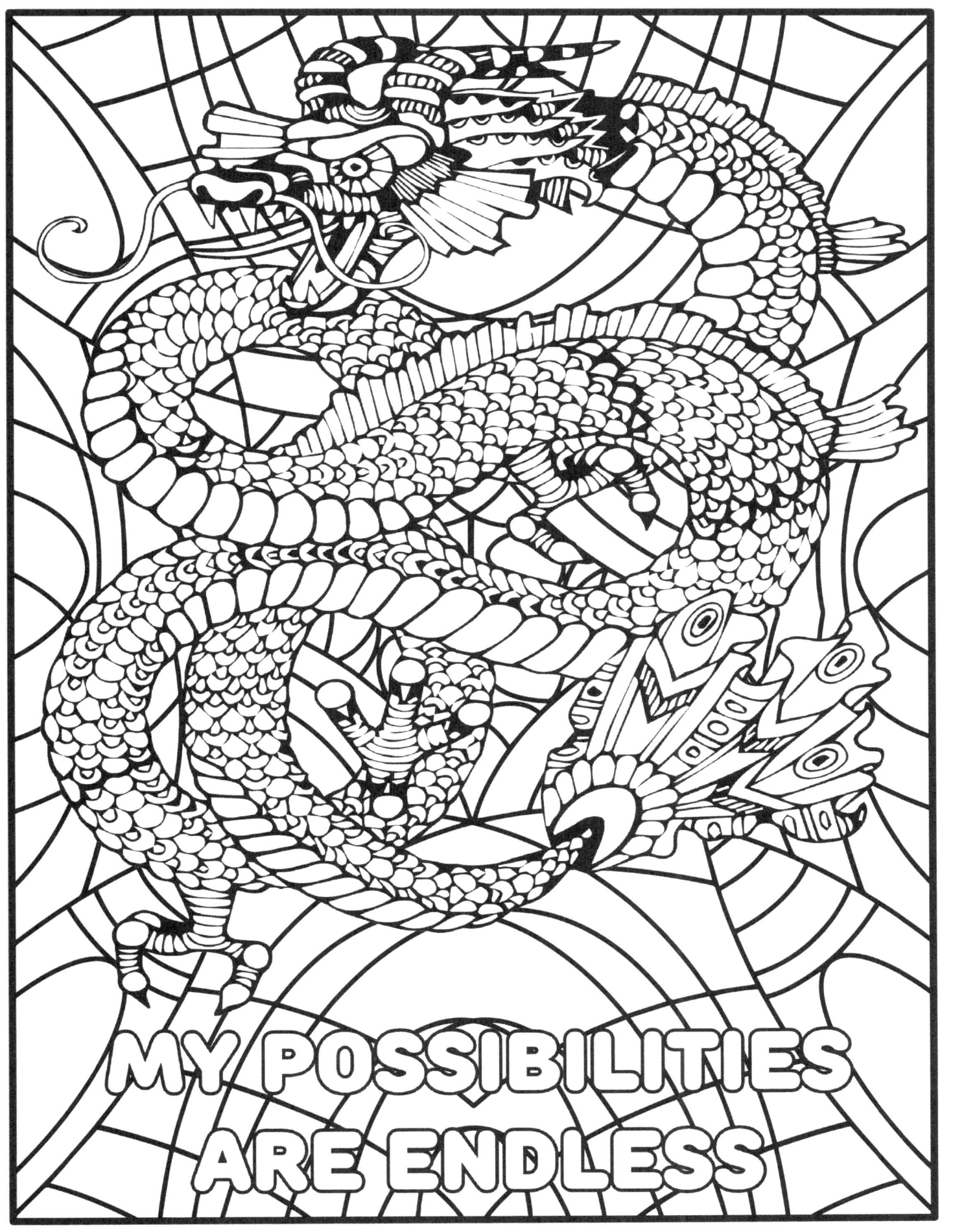

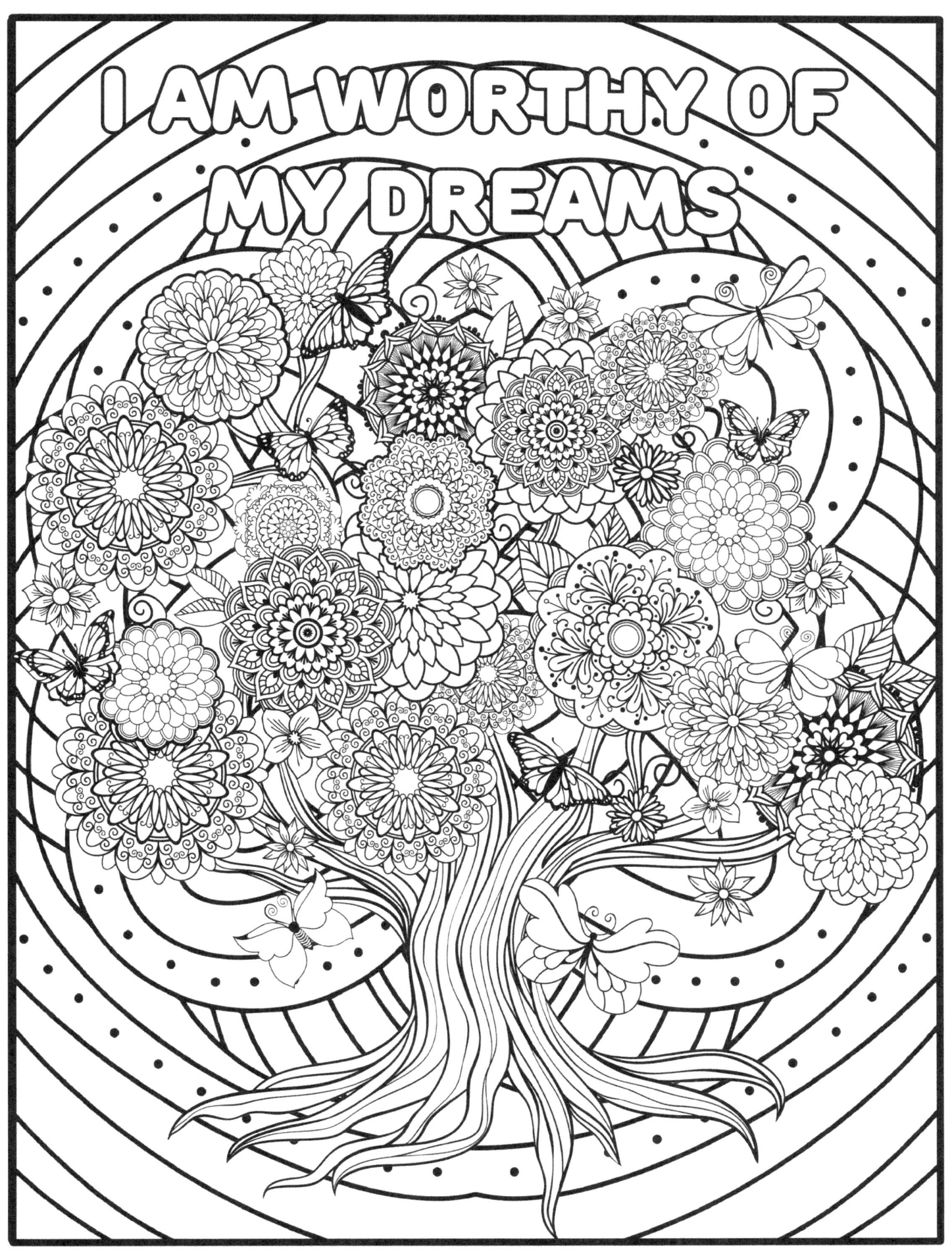

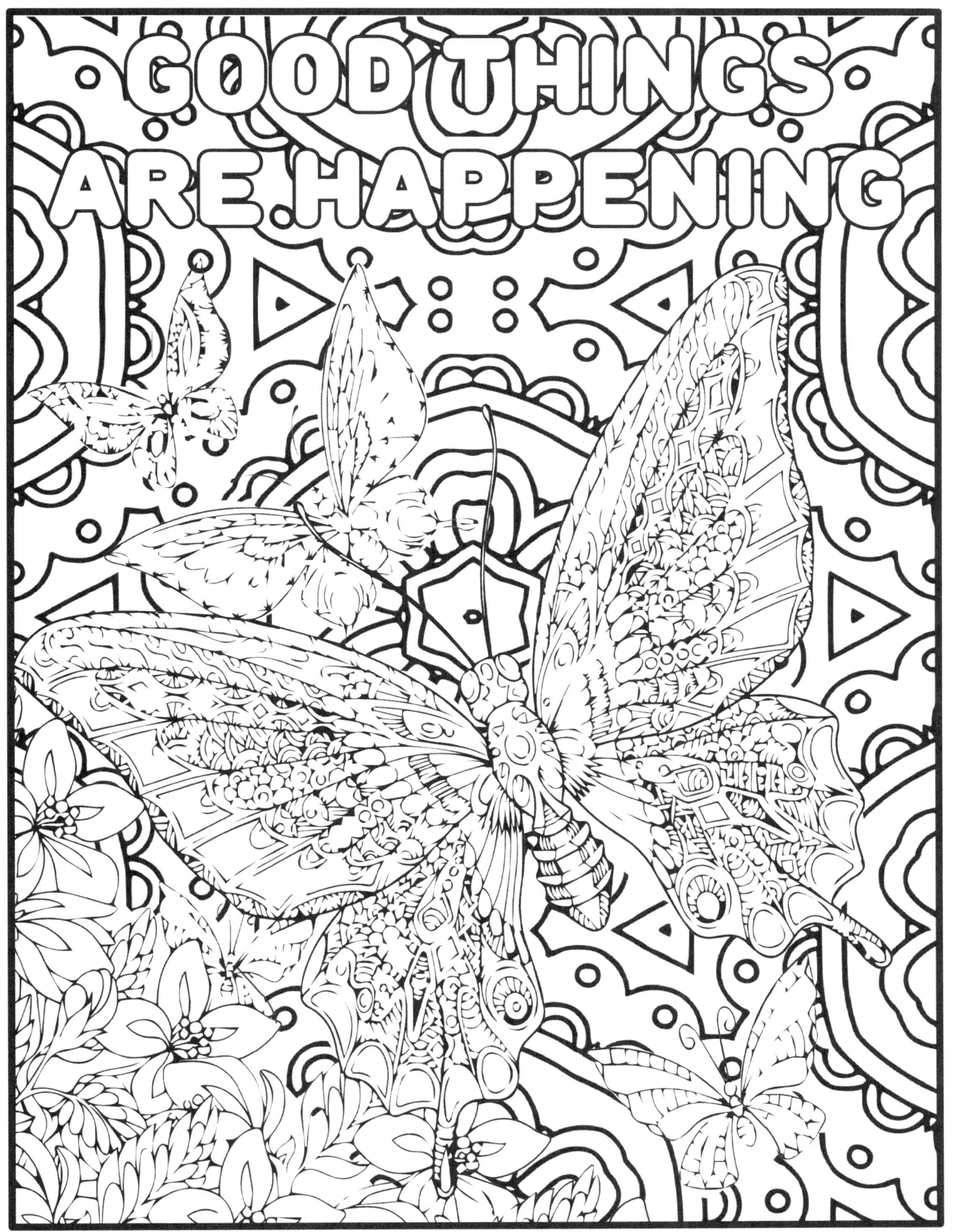

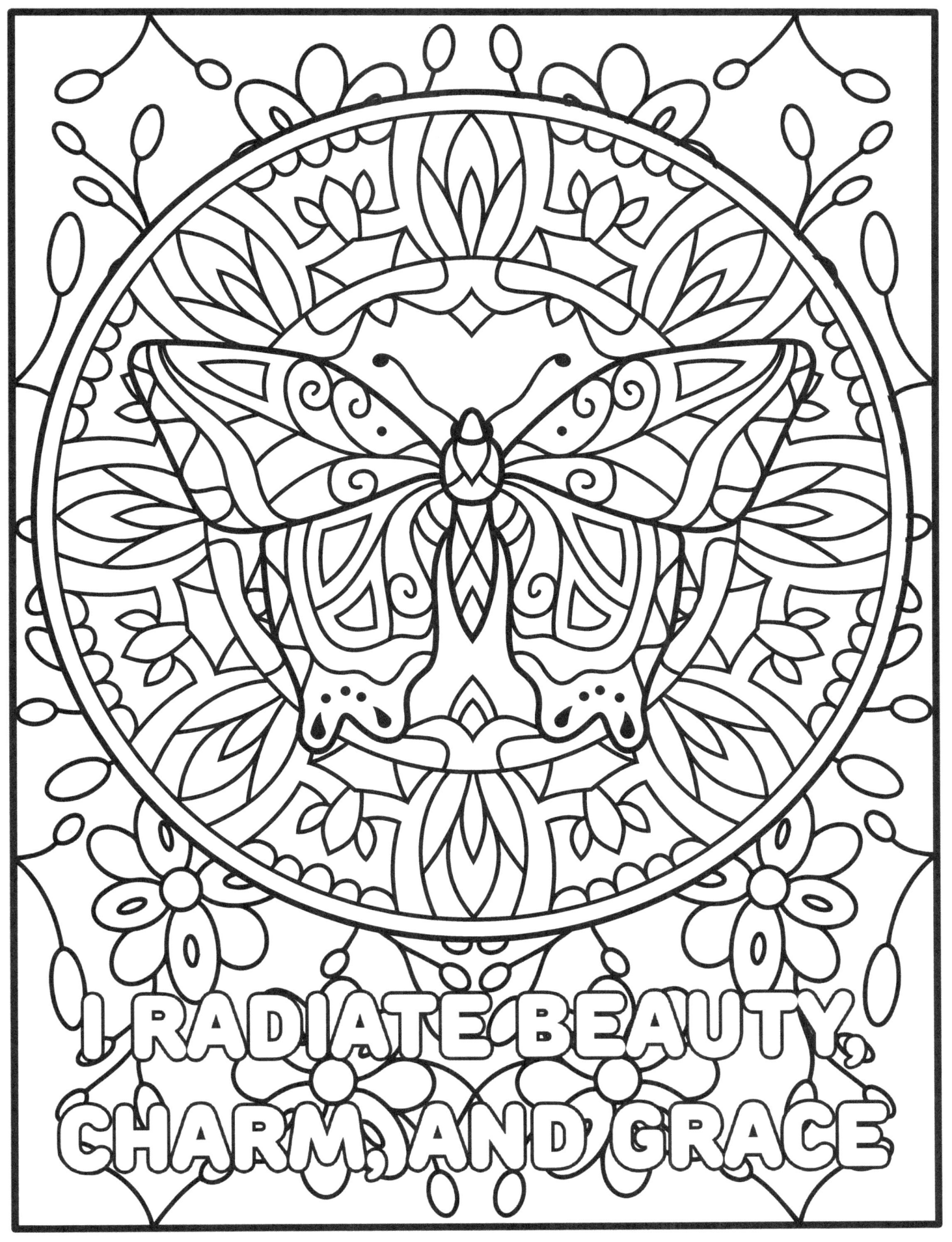

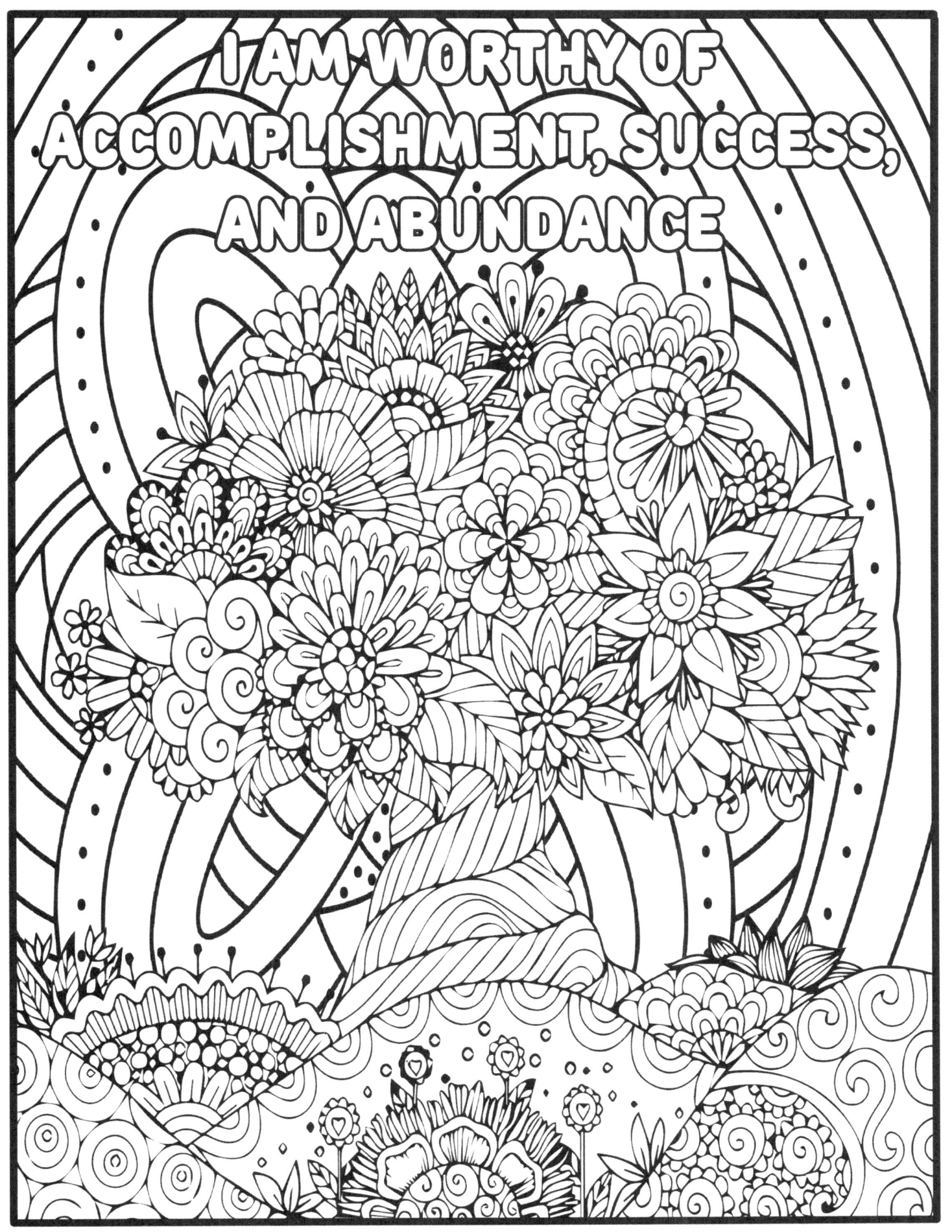

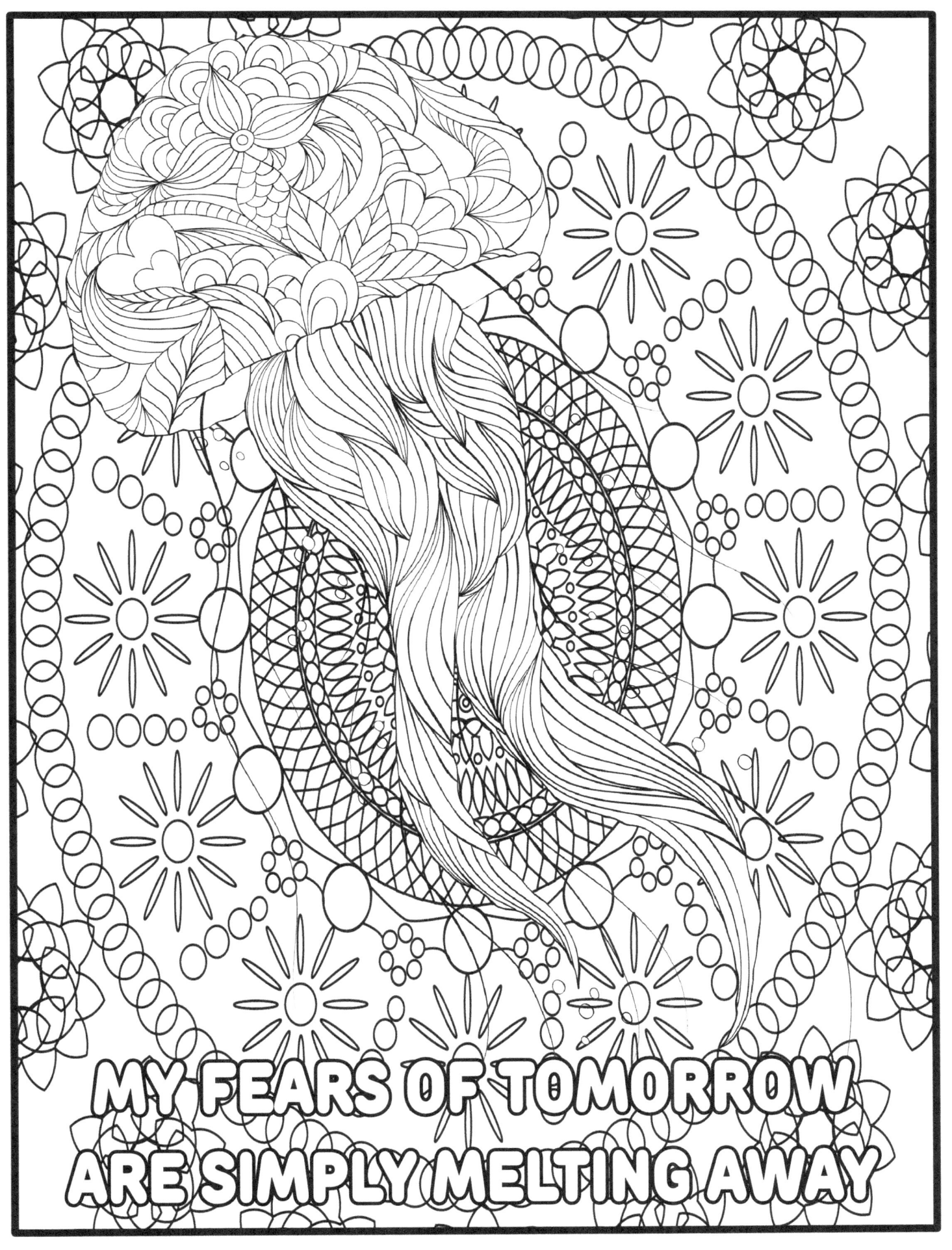

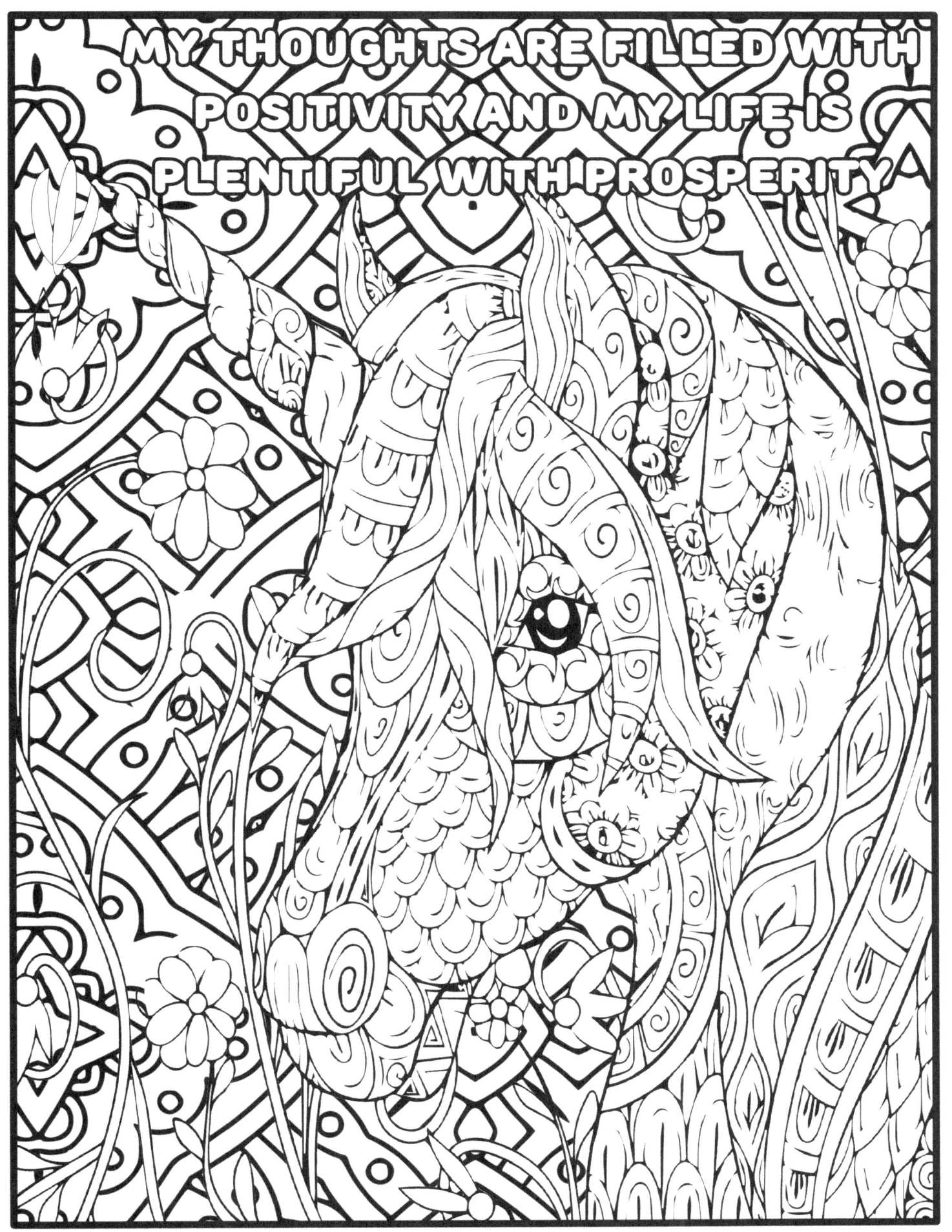

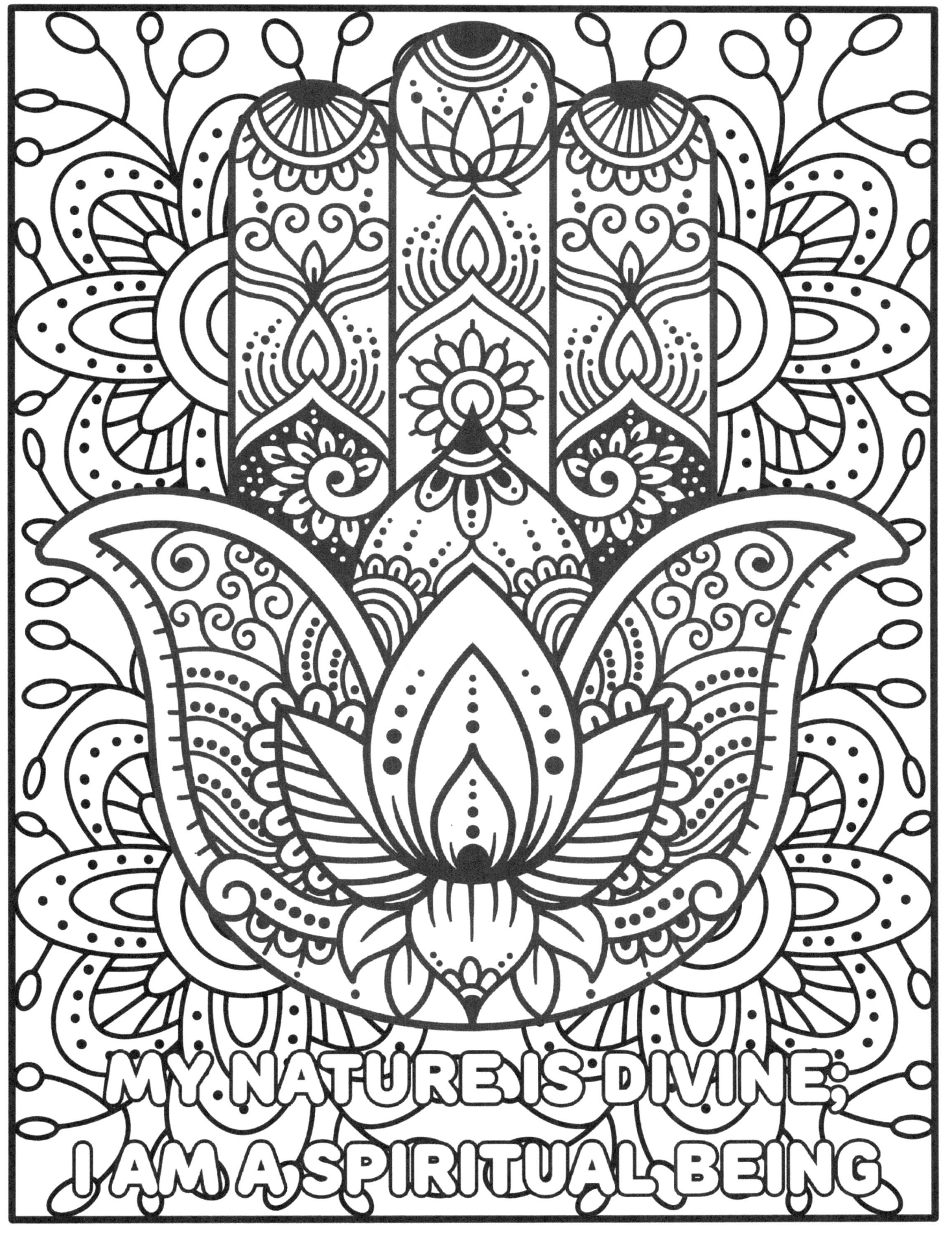

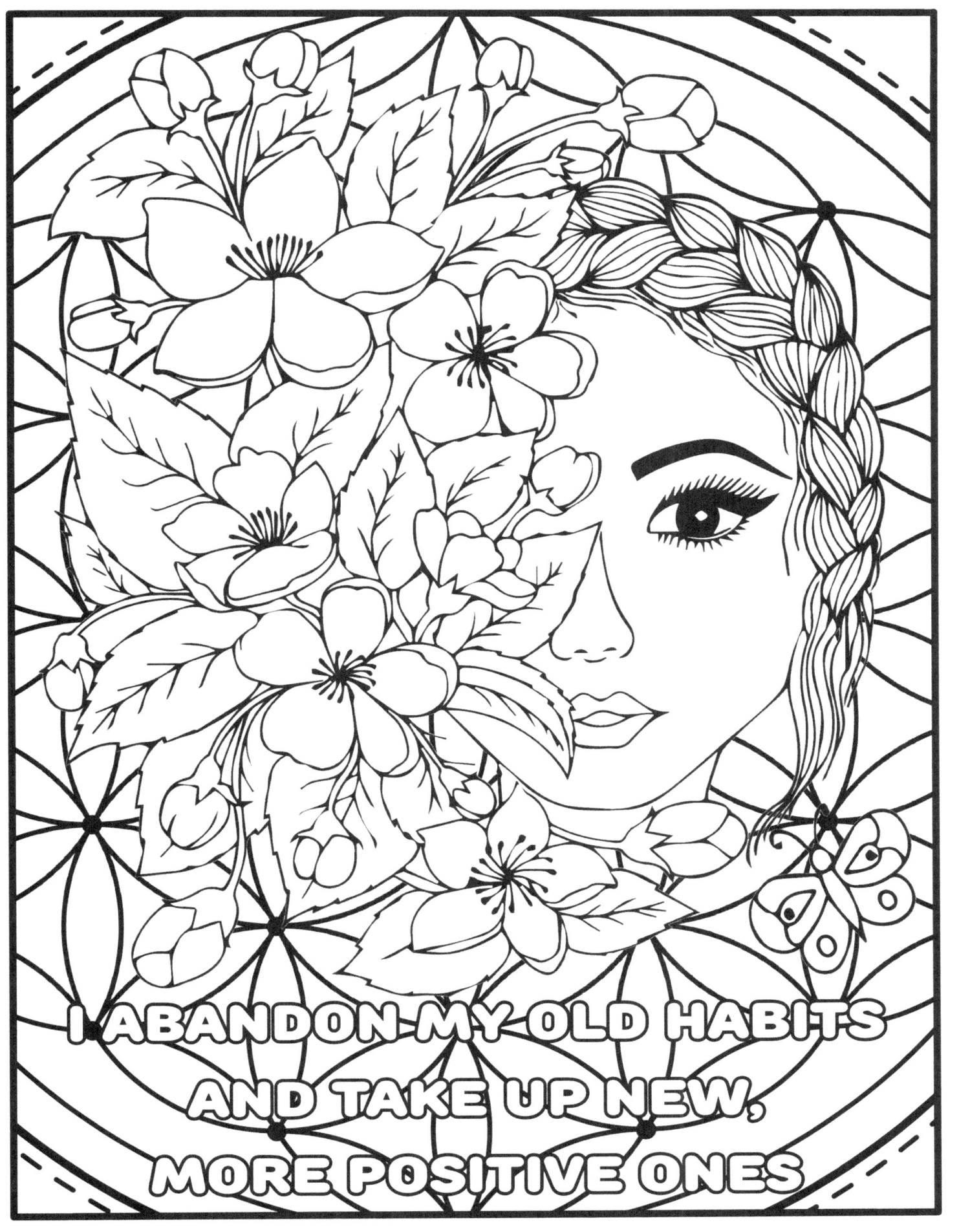

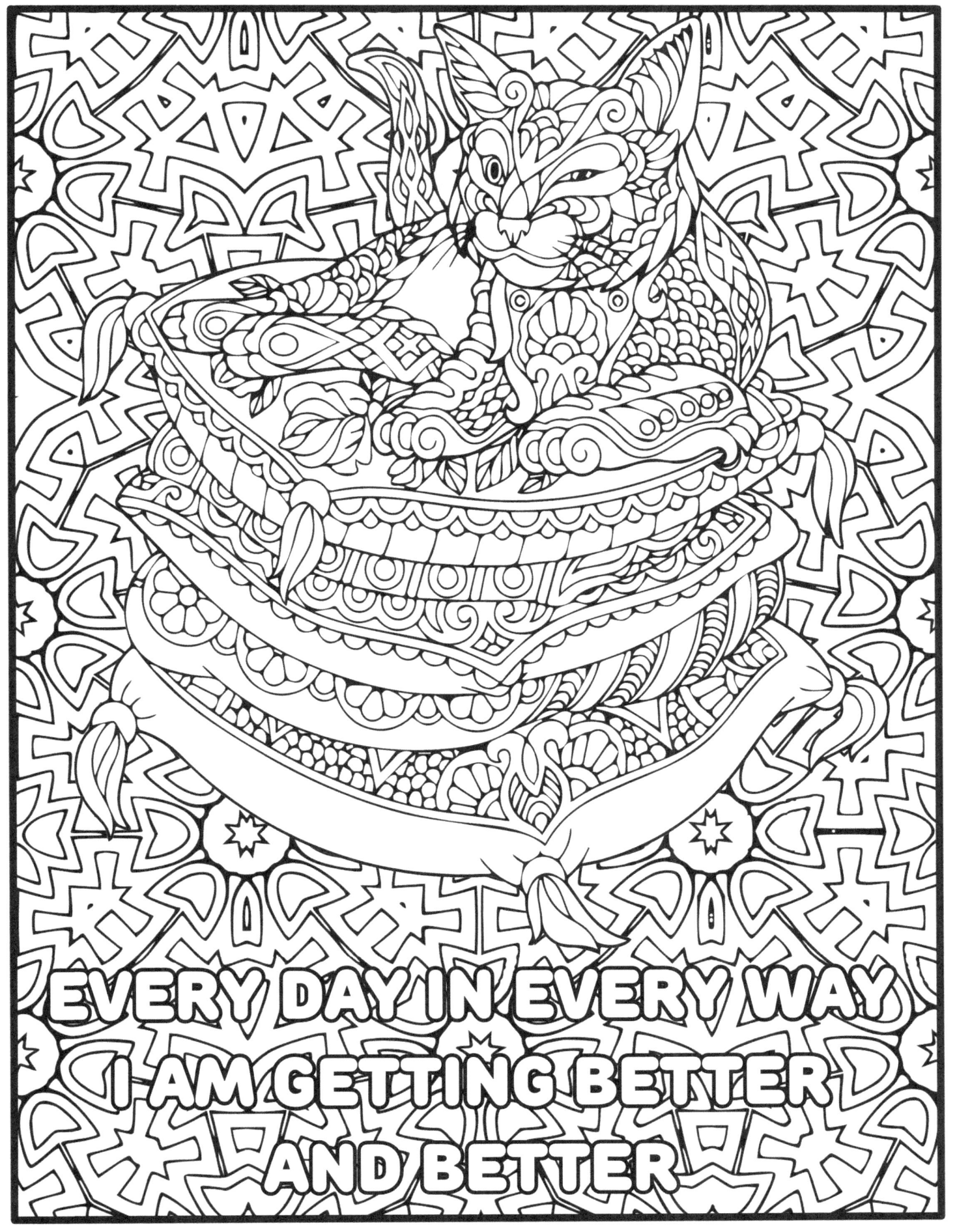

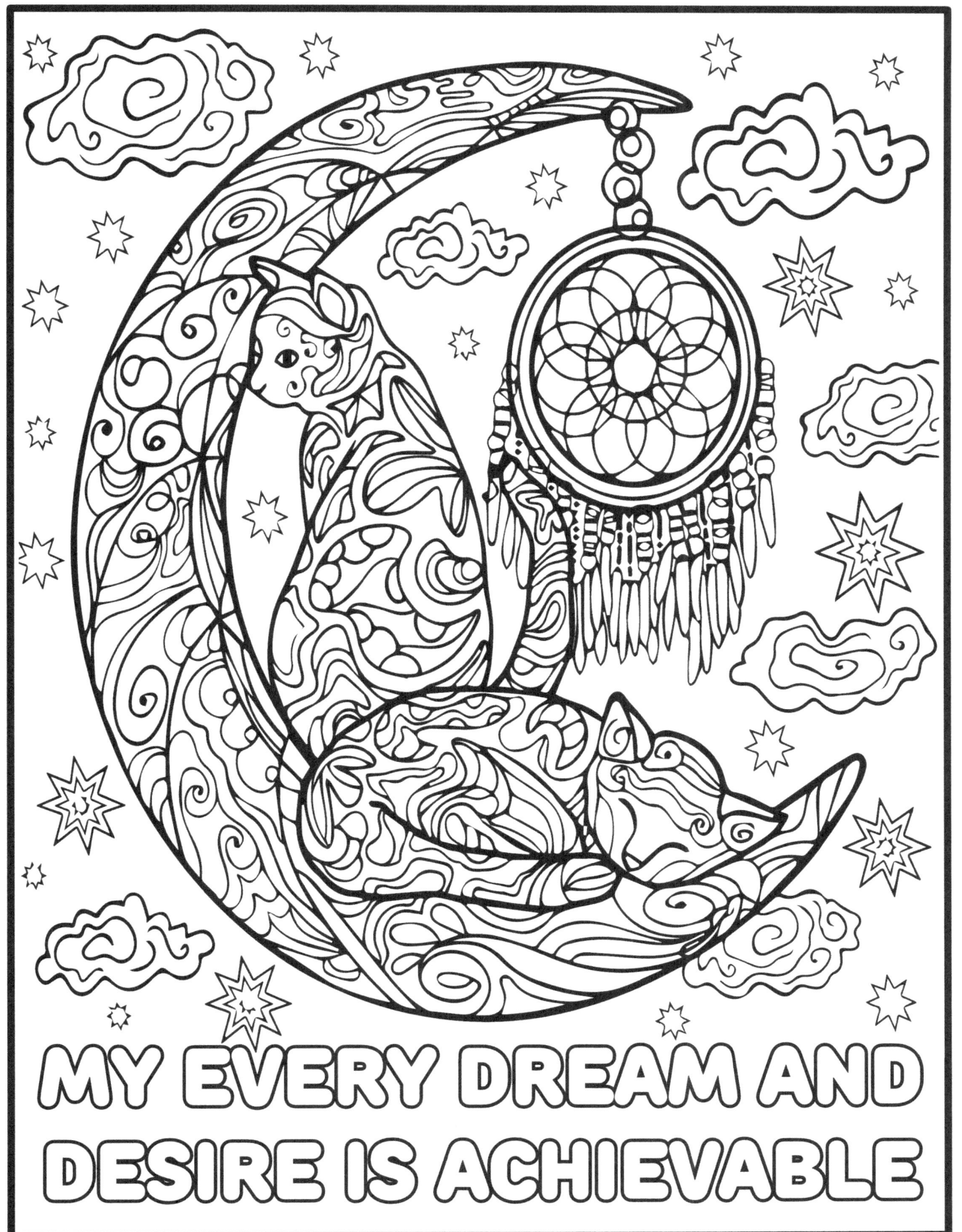

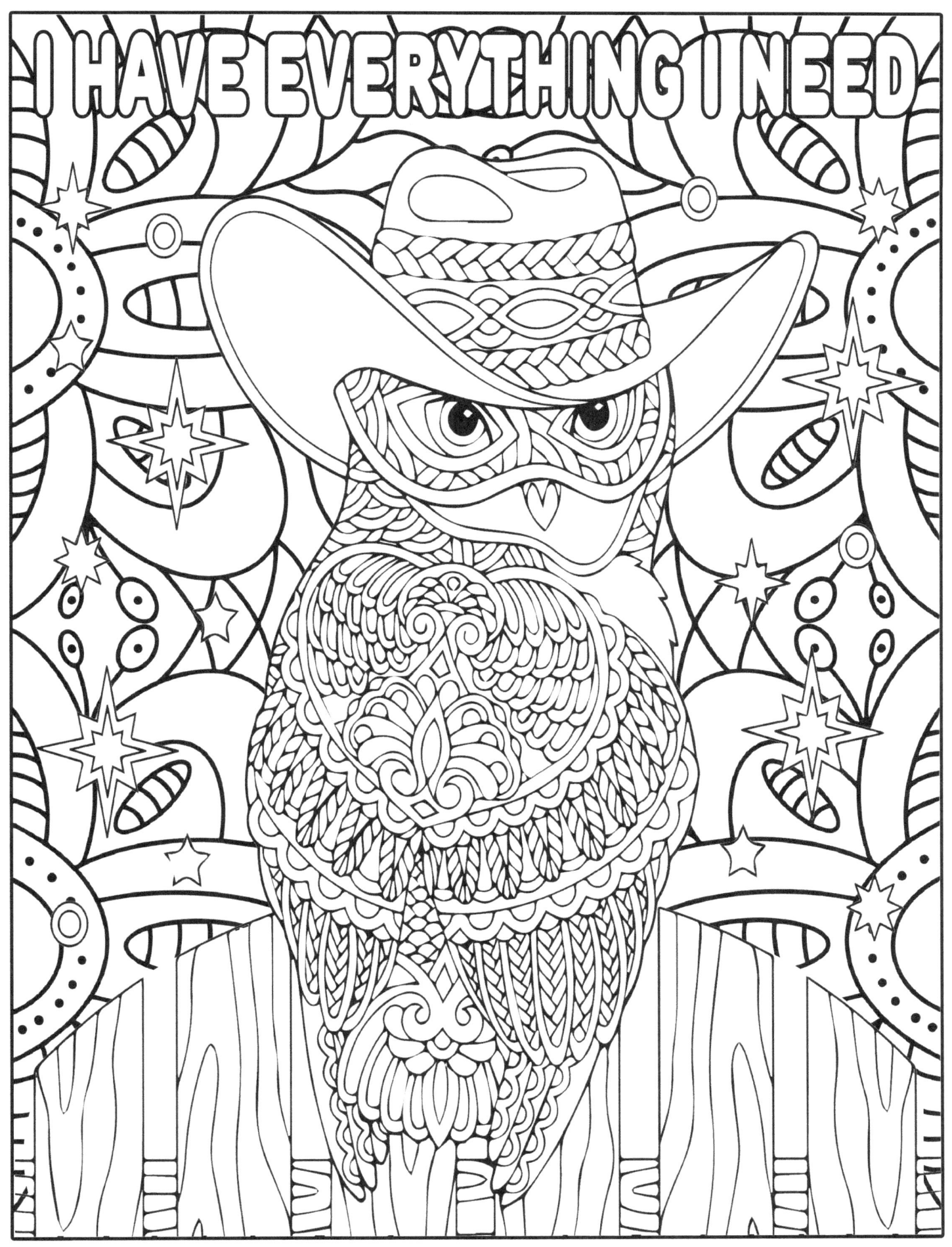

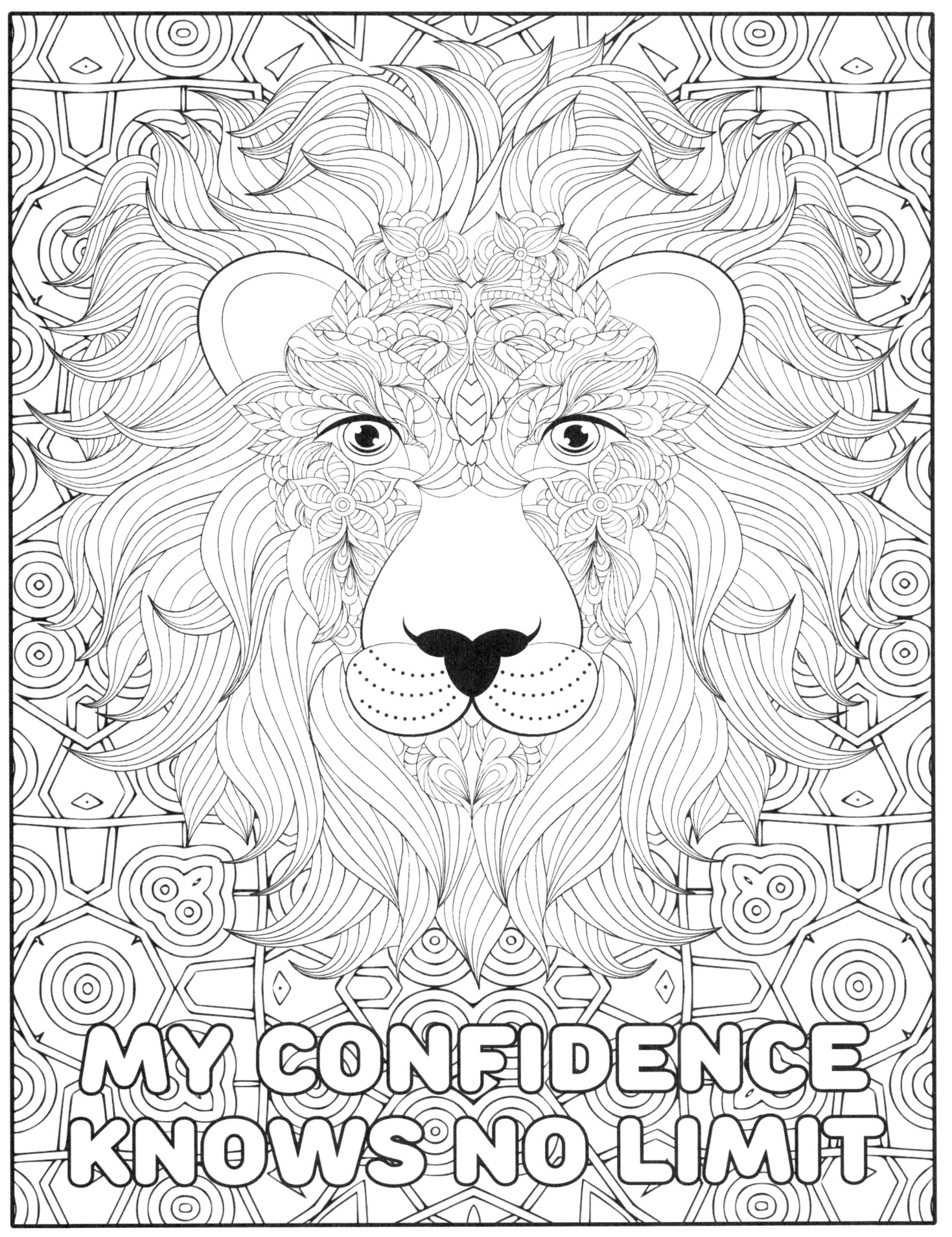

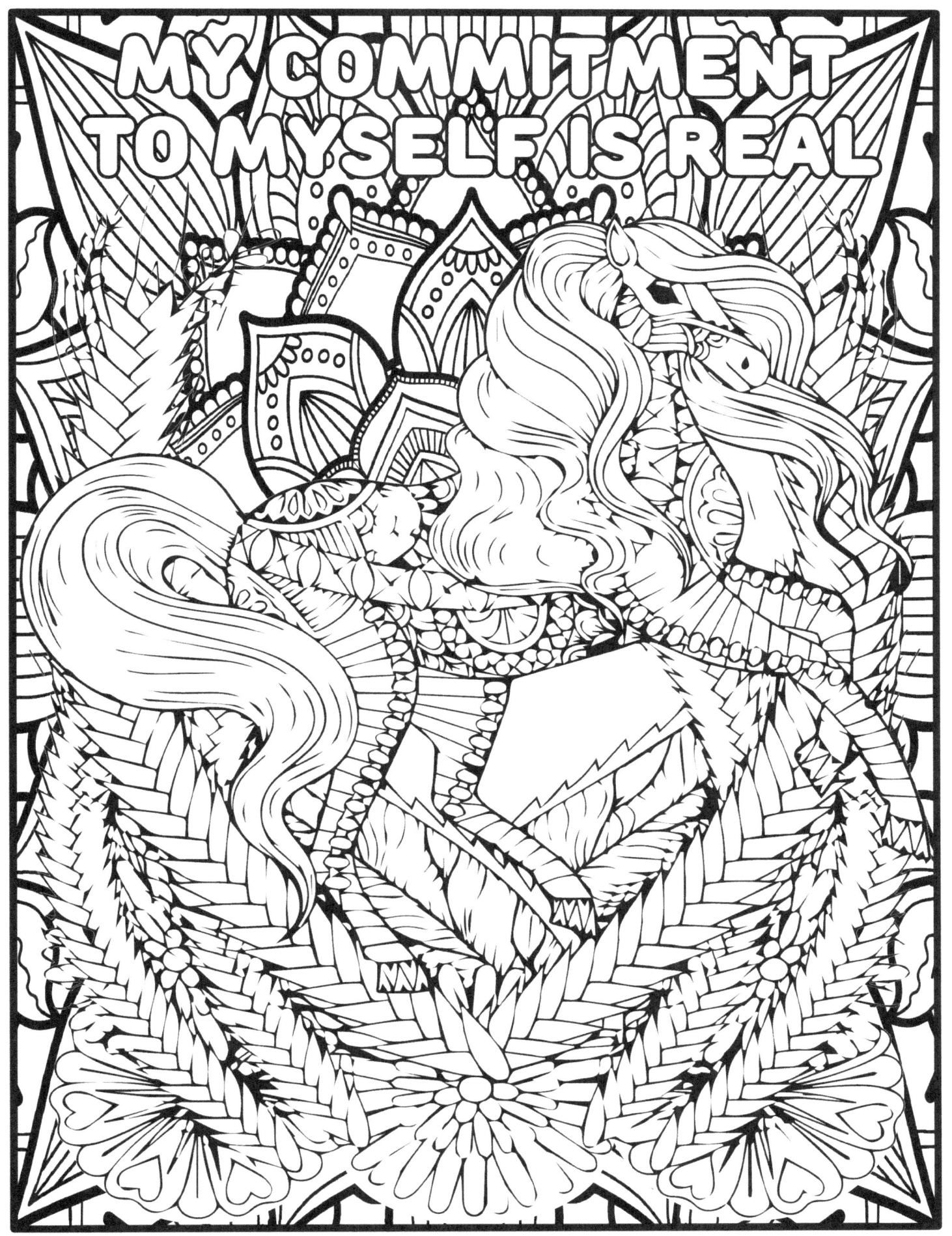

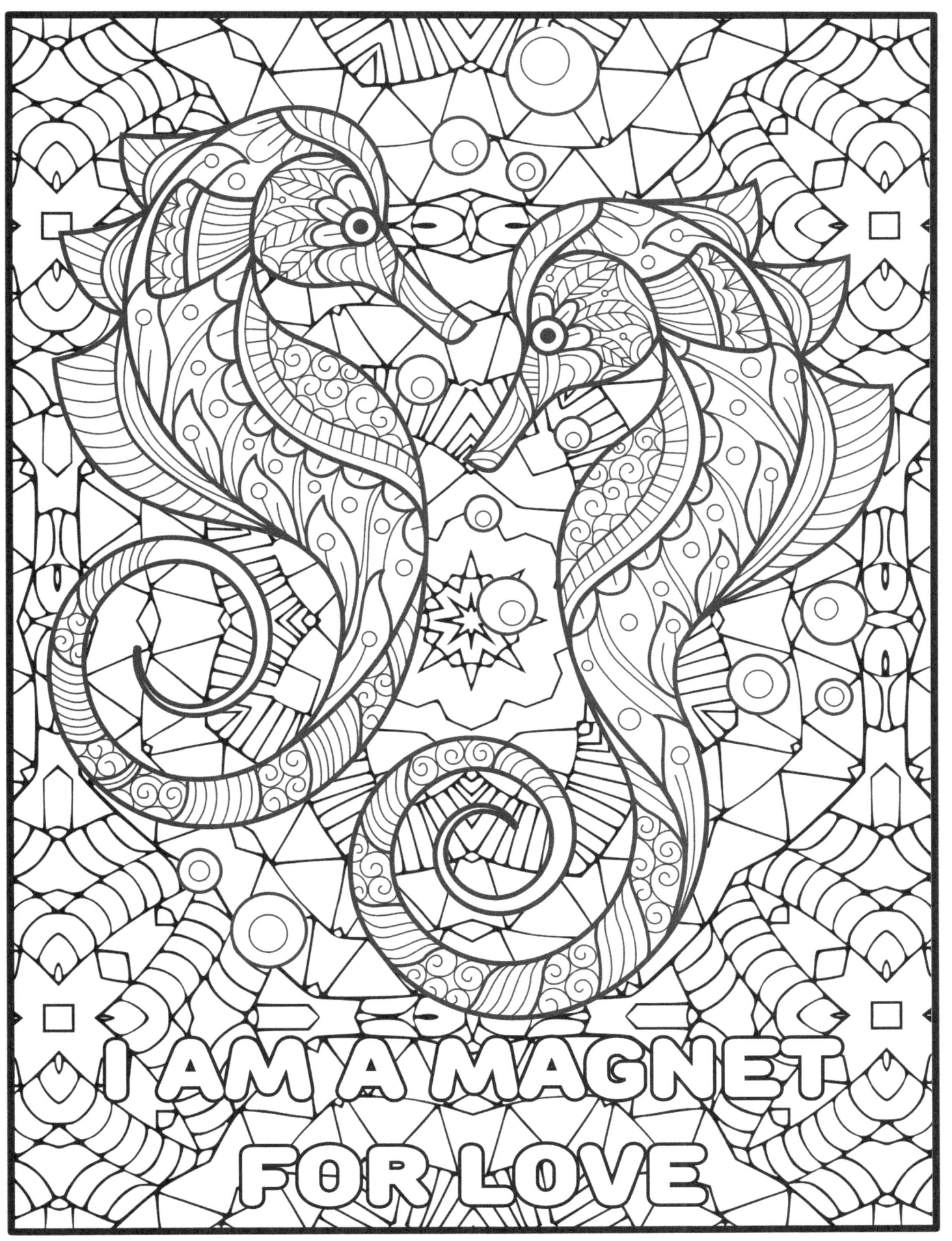

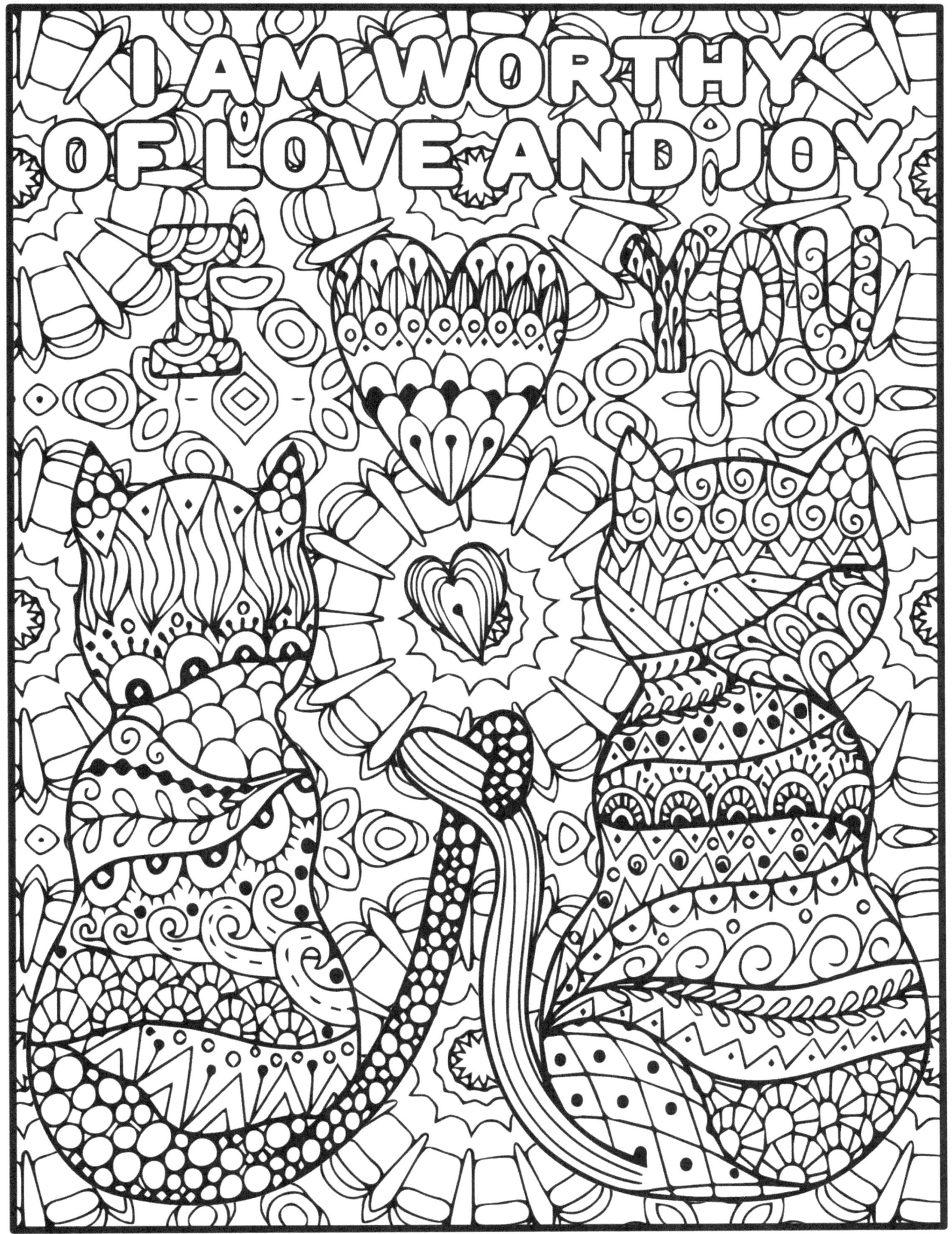

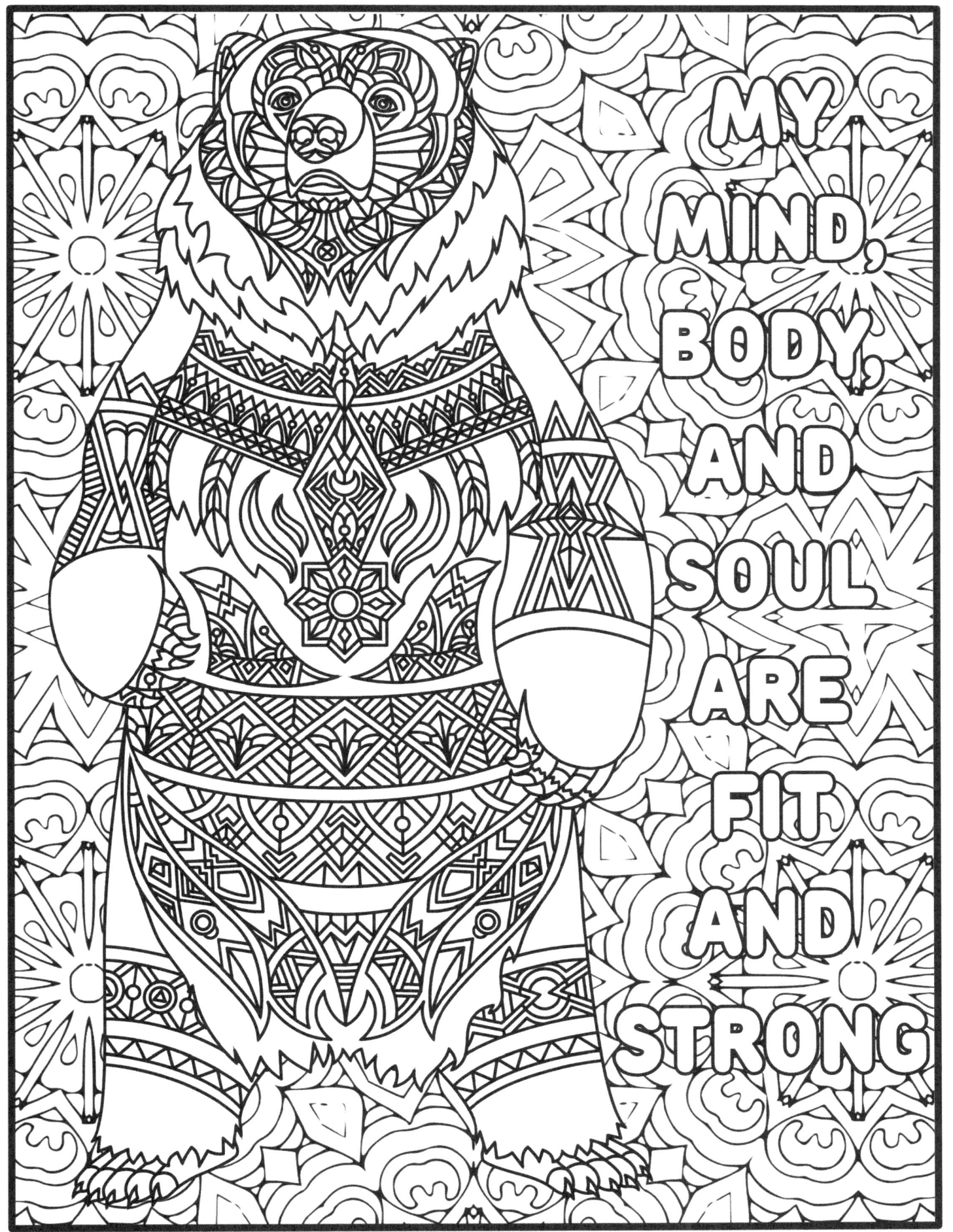

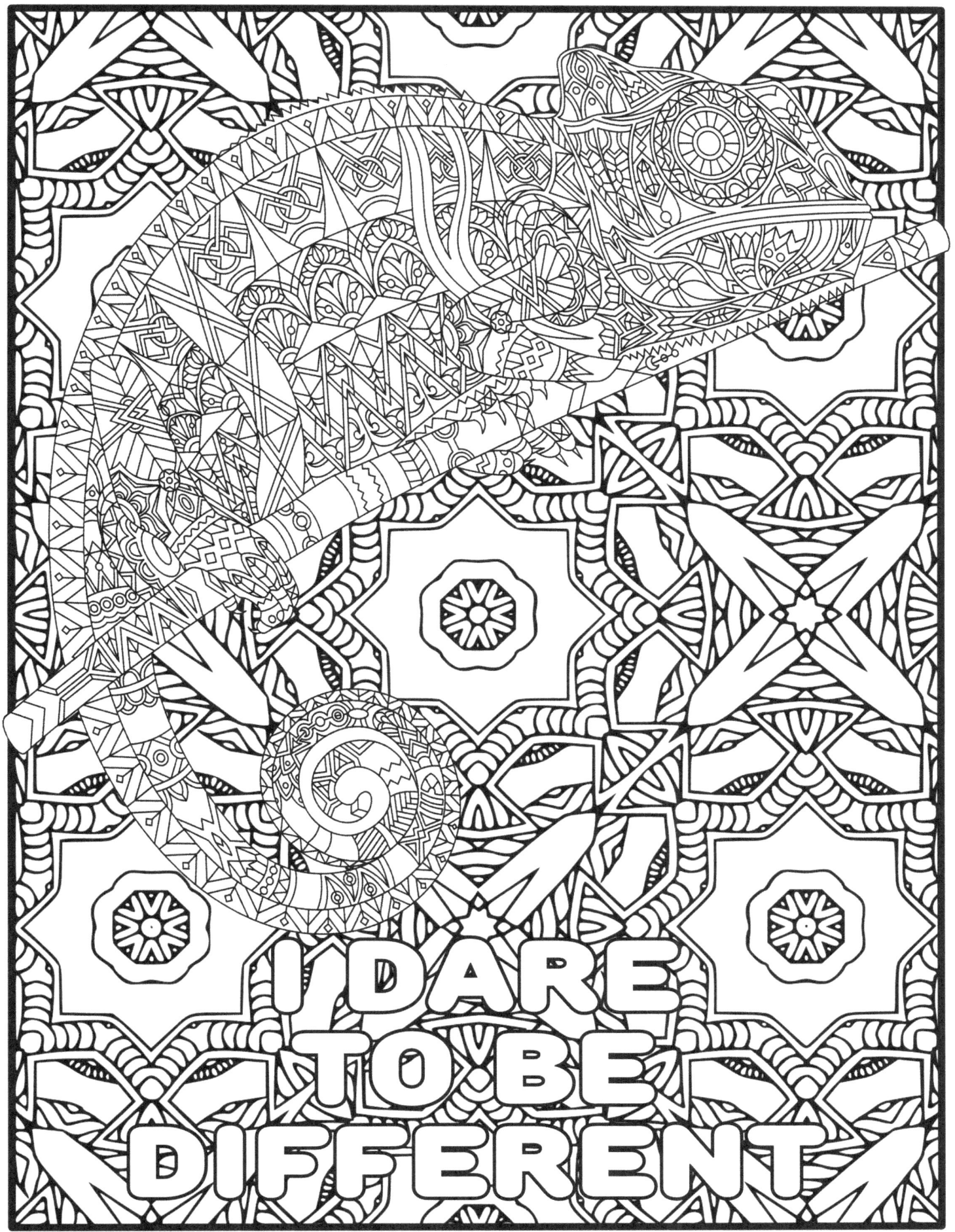

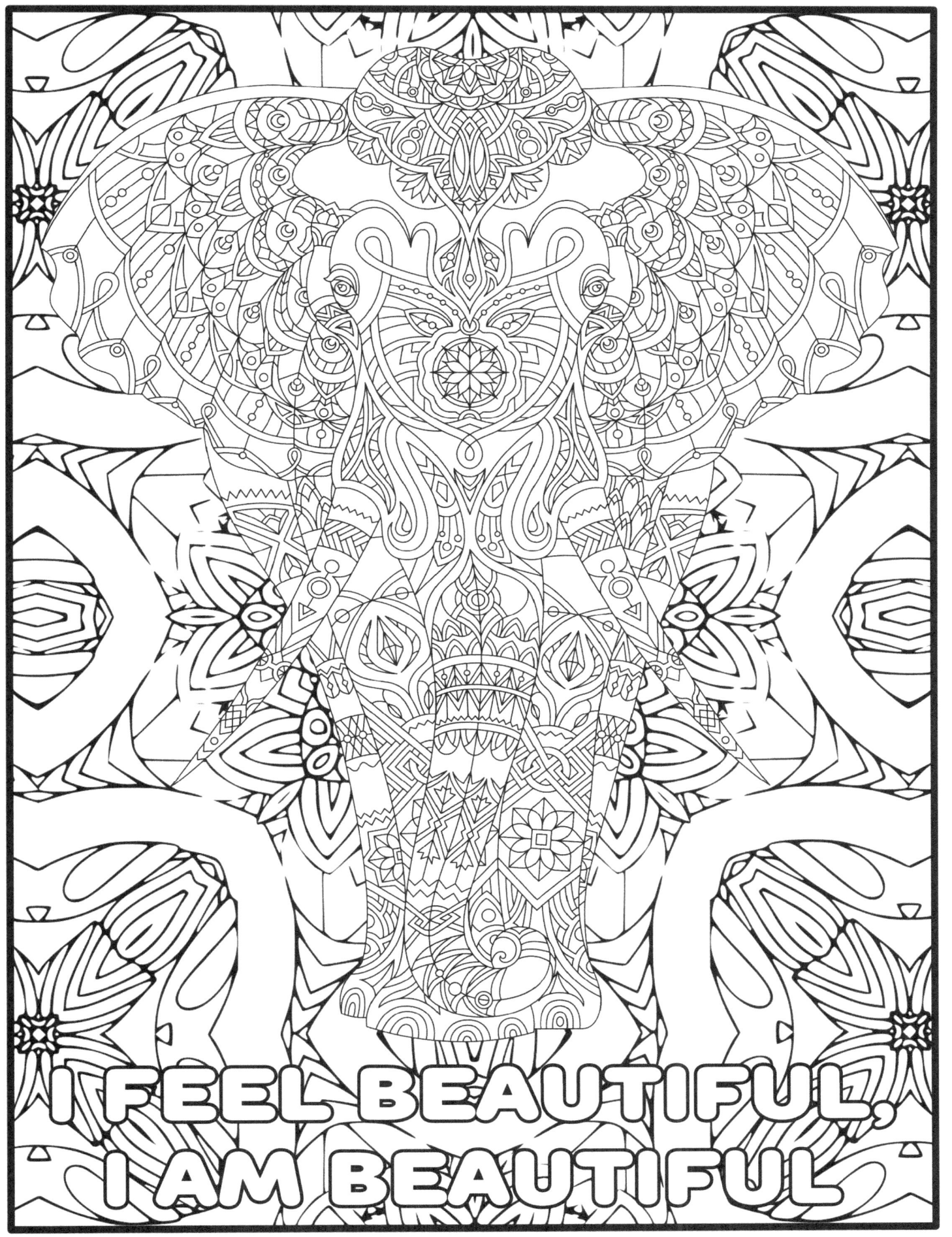

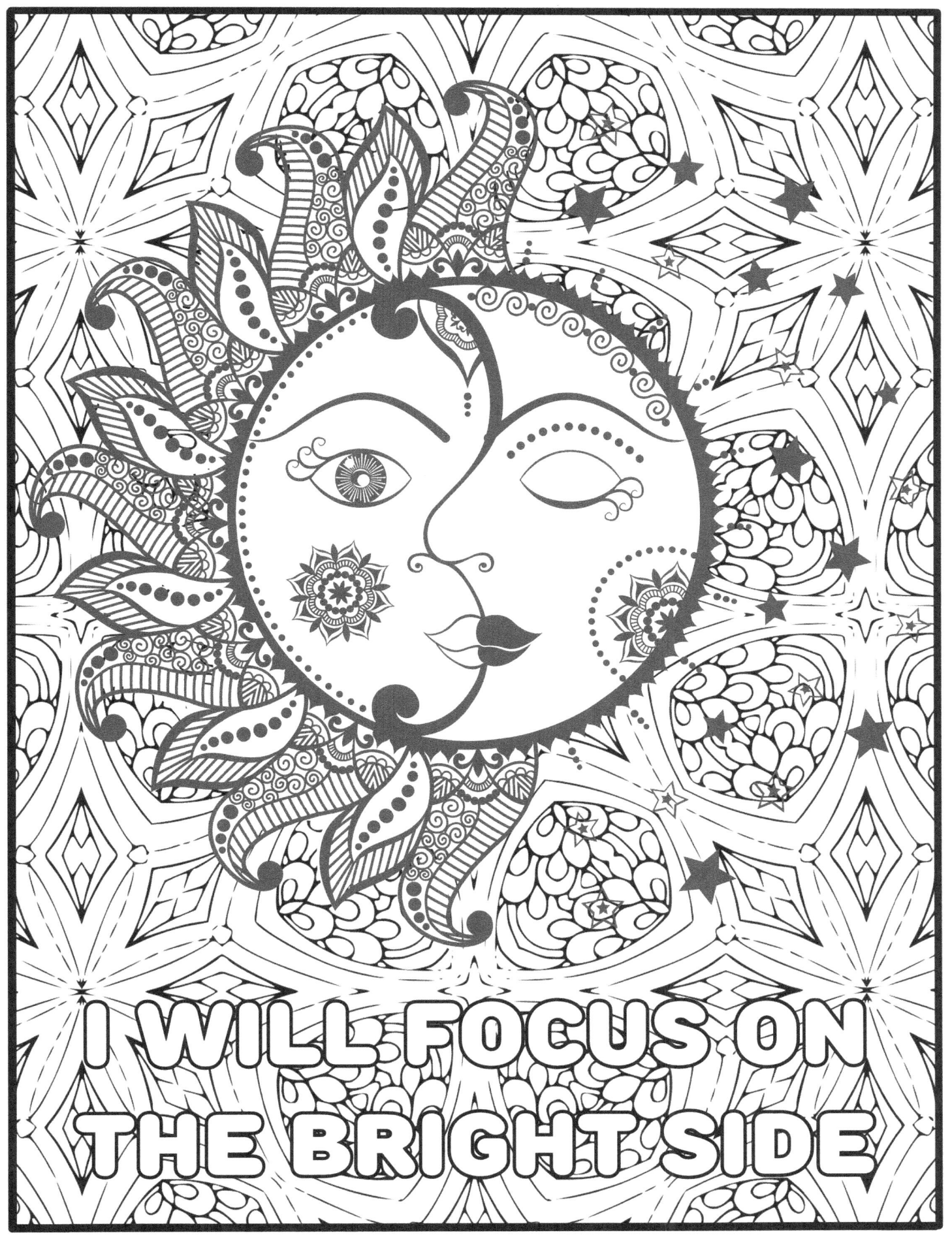

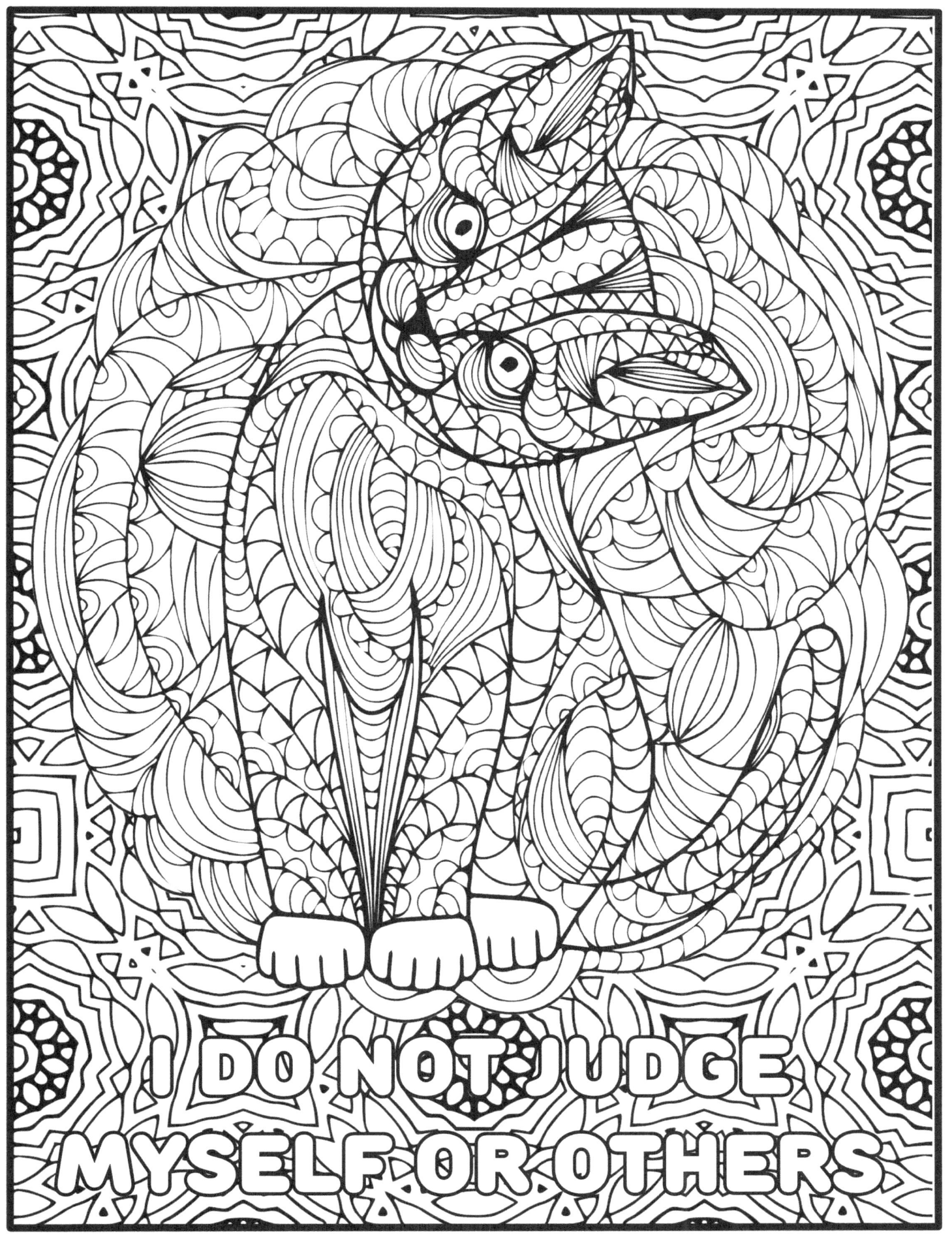

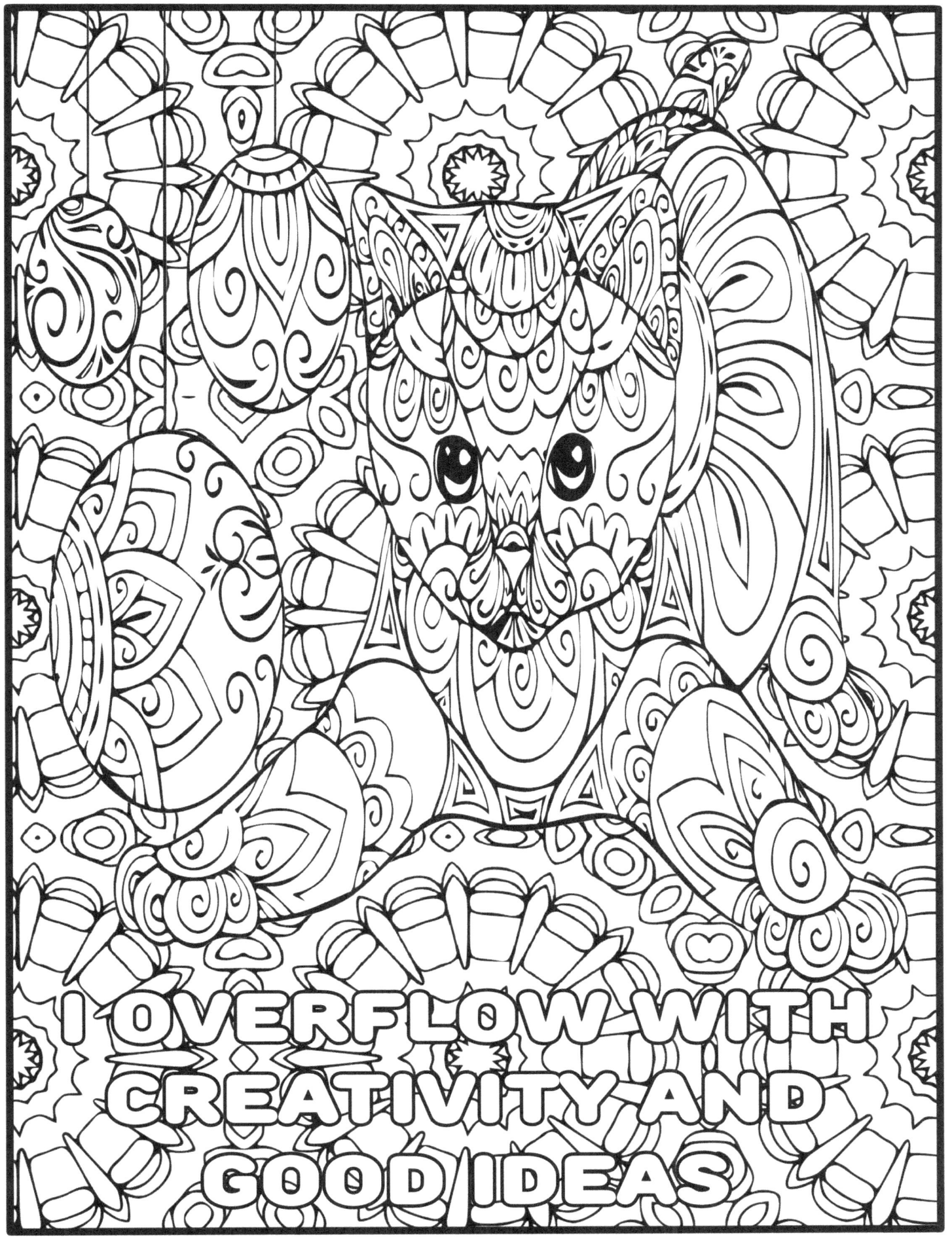

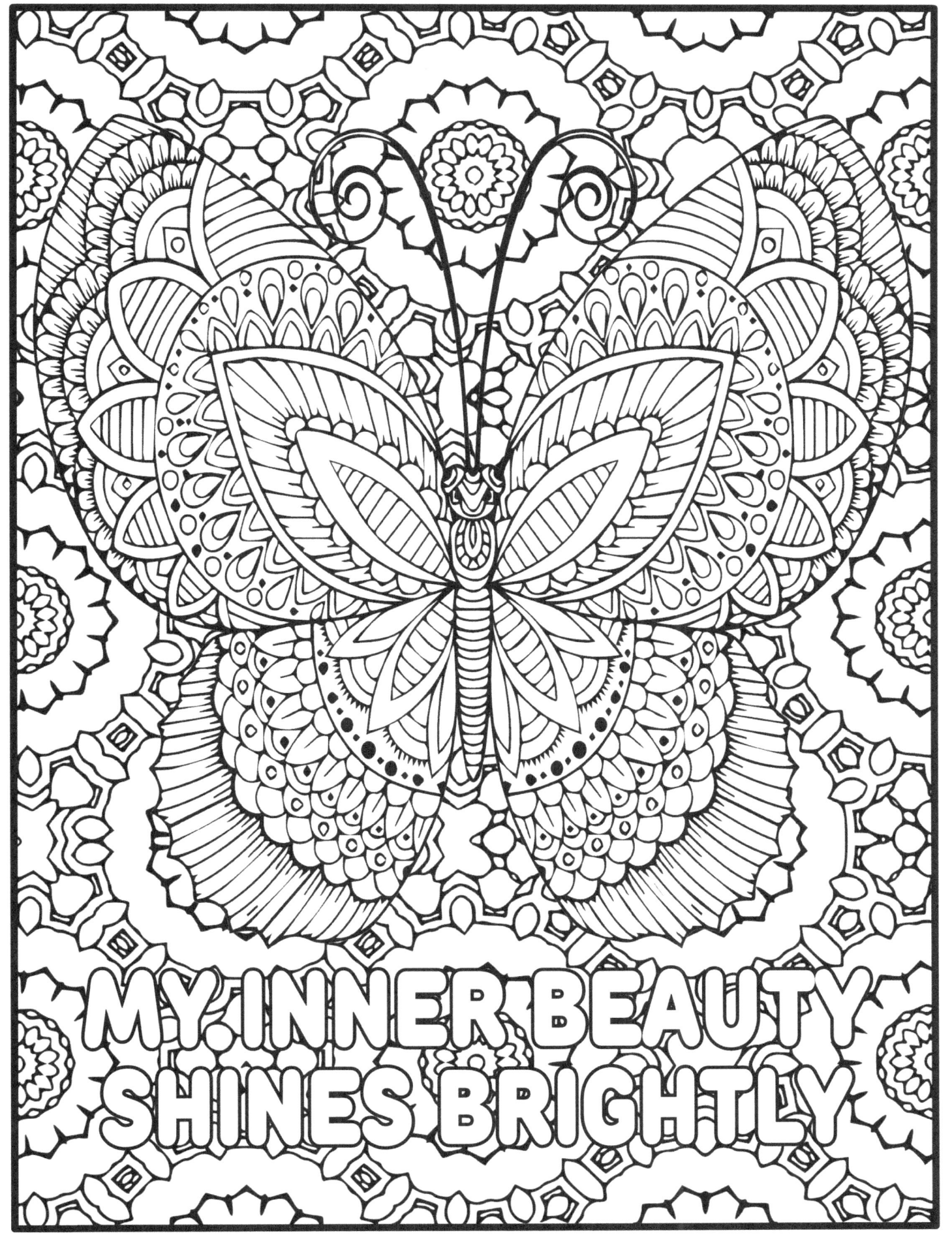

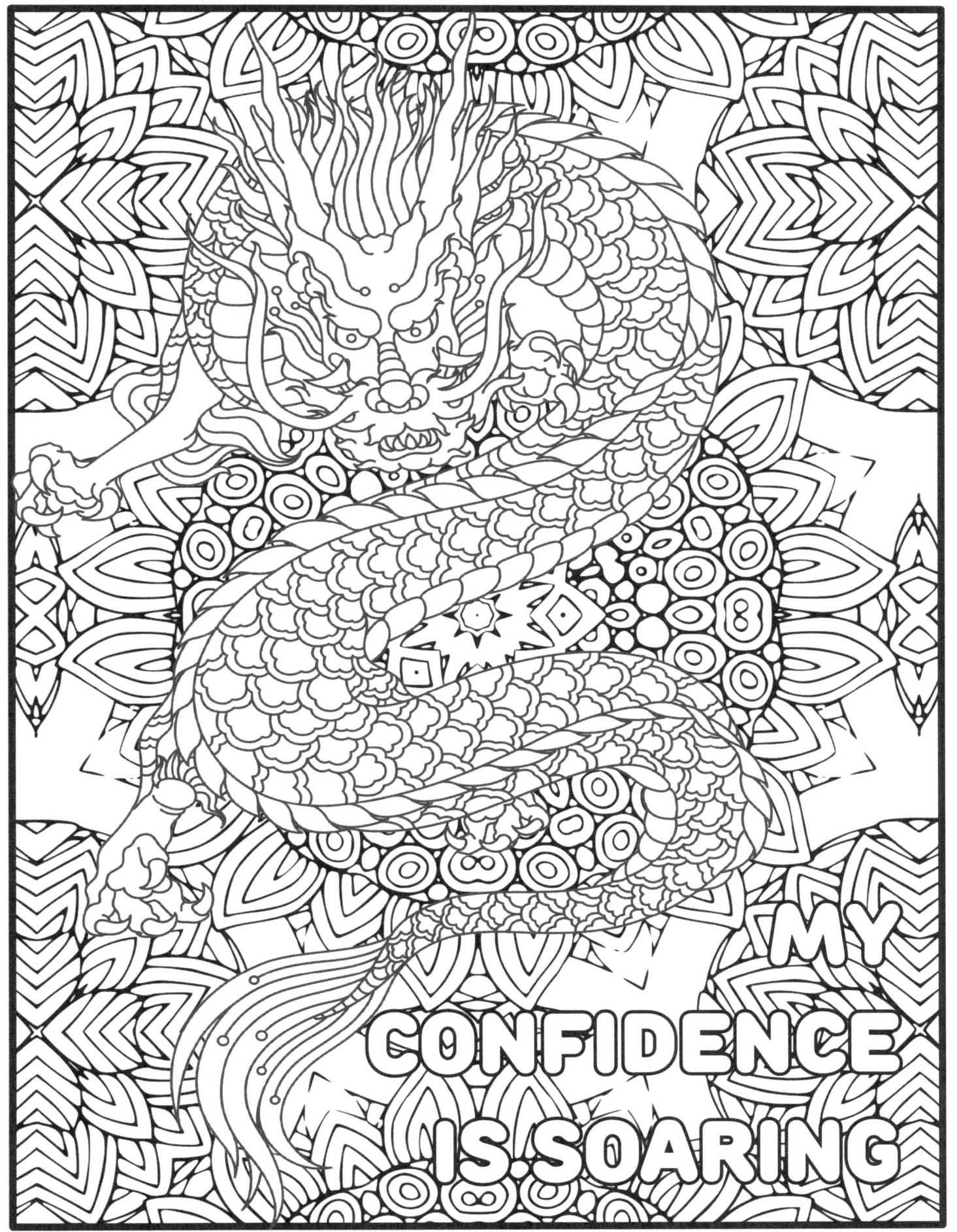

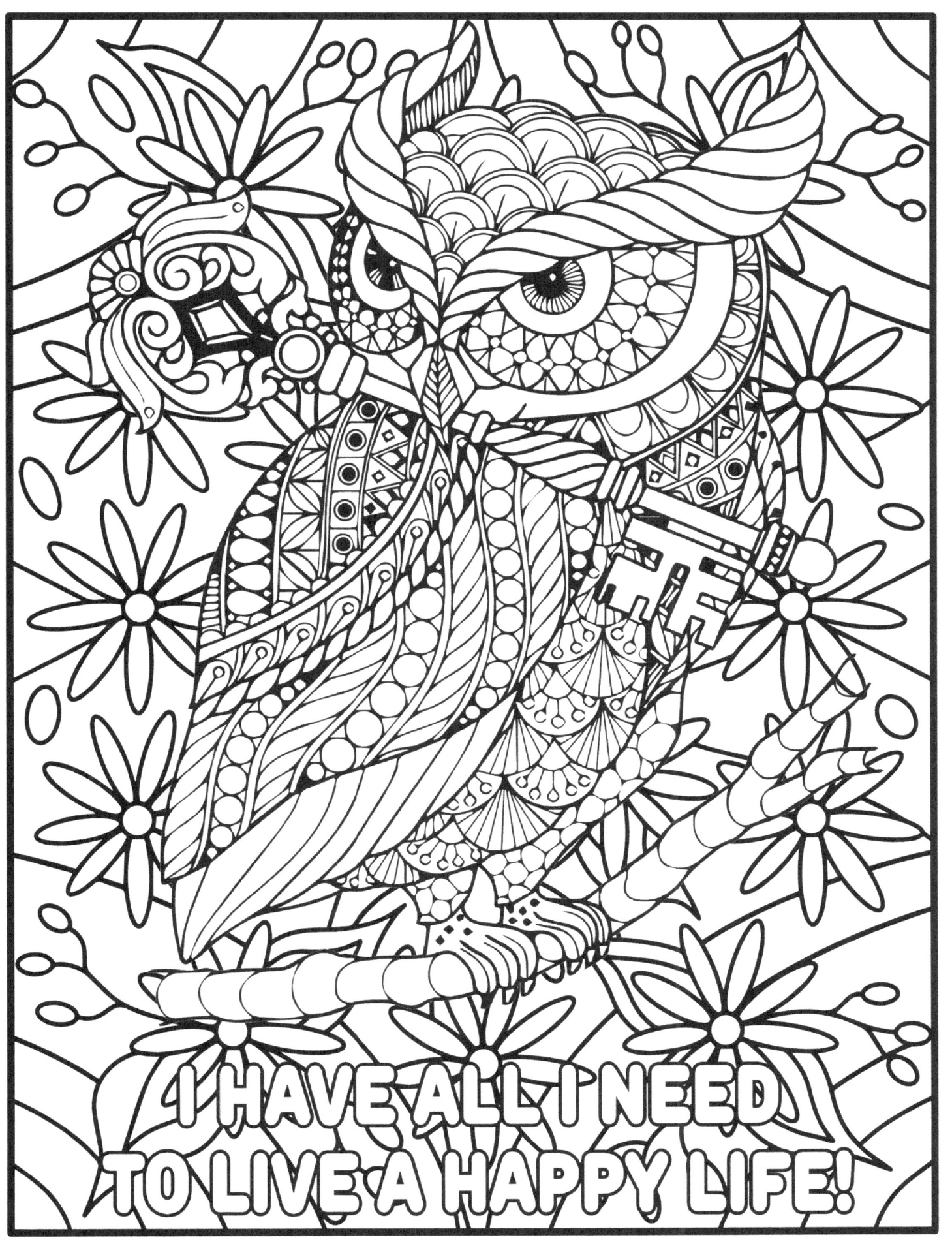

www.ingramcontent.com/pod-product-compliance
Lightning Source LLC
Chambersburg PA
CBHW060438220526
45465CB00008B/3187